Make Your House a Home

Make Your House a Home

This edition published in the UK by Books UK Ltd

Produced by Marshall Cavendish Books, London
(a division of Marshall Cavendish Partworks Ltd), 1997

Copyright © Marshall Cavendish 1997

ISBN 1-871612-54-3

British Library Cataloguing in Publication Data:
A catalogue record for this bookis available from the British Library

Editor-in-chief: Ellen Dupont
Art Editor: Joyce Mason
Editor: Irena Hoare
Production: Craig Chubb

Printed and bound in Malaysia

Some of this material has previously appeared in the
Marshall Cavendish partwork *Get Crafty*

contents

ENLARGING *a design*

If a design you've seen is the wrong size for your purpose there are easy ways to adapt it to your requirements.

USING A PHOTOCOPIER

To work out by how much to enlarge a design, measure the height or the width of the original. Decide on the new size and measure the corresponding height or width.

Calculate the percentage by which you need to enlarge as follows:

$$\frac{\text{new size}}{\text{original size}} \times 100 = \text{percentage required}$$

for example:

$$\frac{12}{8} \times 100 = 150\%$$

Most photocopiers only go up to 200 percent, so copy the original in two stages. Copy it at 200 percent, then enlarge it again, using this size in relation to the final size required.

USING A SIMPLE GRID SYSTEM

You will need pencil, paper, ruler, masking tape, tracing and graph paper. You can either draw a grid directly on the original pattern or copy it on to tracing paper first. Draw a grid on the pattern or on tracing paper, dividing the total area into squares. Then draw a second grid, this time to the size required and divide it into the same number of squares as the original. The design is then drawn square by square on to the new grid.

HOW TO ENLARGE AND REDUCE A DESIGN ON A GRID

HOW TO ENLARGE

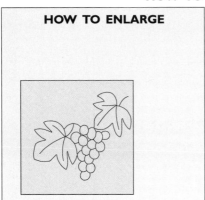

1 *Although you can draw a grid on the original if you prefer, it's easier if you copy it. To do this fix tracing paper to it with masking tape. Copy the pattern on to this so you can use it for a grid.*

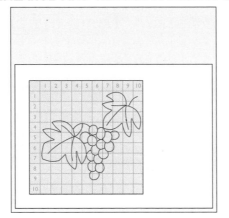

2 *Place a sheet of graph paper under the tracing paper and use it as guide to draw a square or rectangular outline around the design. Divide this into squares and number them.*

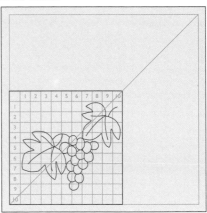

3 *Align the bottom left-hand corner of the design with a larger sheet of tracing paper. Draw a second rectangle the size you want by extending the two sides and the diagonal.*

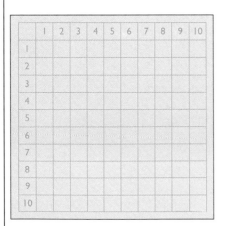

4 *Use the graph paper as a guide to divide the rectangle into the same number of squares as the first grid and number them correspondingly.*

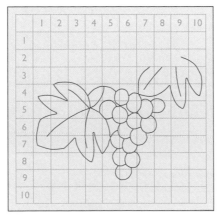

5 *Using the first grid as a guide, copy the design, square by square, on to the larger grid, using the numbers as guide to complete each square.*

HOW TO REDUCE

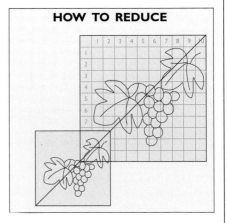

To reduce a design, draw a smaller rectangle, divide it into squares and number them. Transfer the design, square by square, using the numbers as a guide.

chapter one

INTRODUCING COLOUR

We are surrounded by colour yet few of us really understand it. By learning the basic principles, we can feel confident about using colour and put colour schemes together successfully.

Colour affects every part of our lives. It influences our moods, emotions and even the way we perceive proportions. A source of inspiration to artists and craftspeople, colour can also be quite daunting in its variety.

Everywhere we look there are colours, both natural and created by man, and they exist in a bewildering range of combinations. Think of all the colours a leaf goes through from spring to autumn, or the shades of terracotta in an old brick wall.

THE COLOUR WHEEL

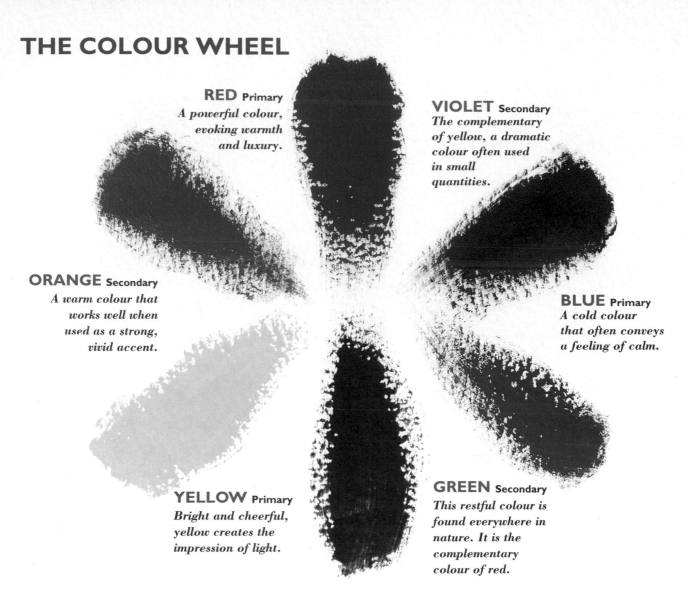

RED Primary
A powerful colour, evoking warmth and luxury.

VIOLET Secondary
The complementary of yellow, a dramatic colour often used in small quantities.

ORANGE Secondary
A warm colour that works well when used as a strong, vivid accent.

BLUE Primary
A cold colour that often conveys a feeling of calm.

YELLOW Primary
Bright and cheerful, yellow creates the impression of light.

GREEN Secondary
This restful colour is found everywhere in nature. It is the complementary colour of red.

All the colours we see are, in fact, the colours in the rainbow. To show how colours relate to each other, designers often use the colour wheel, a rainbow arranged as a circle.

This simple colour wheel shows both primary and secondary colours. Primary colours are the three basic colours: red, blue and yellow. All other colours are made up of combinations of these three colours.

Mixing two primary colours produces a new colour referred to as a secondary colour – red mixed with yellow creates orange, yellow and blue make green and red mixed with blue creates violet.

The colour wheel is arranged so that complementary, or contrasting, colours such as blue and orange, are placed opposite each other. Such colours are best used sparingly for striking effects. True complementary colours may vibrate when used together in almost equal amounts, which can be difficult on the eye.

Harmonious colours lie next to each other on the wheel. They usually look well when used together in muted combinations.

WARM AND COOL COLOURS

The colour wheel also distinguishes between warm and cool colours. Reds, oranges and yellows are all warm colours. They create an effect that can be uplifting or cosy. Green and blue are cool colours and are often used to promote a tranquil, soothing effect.

The best way to handle colour with confidence is to feel familiar with it. Make a mental note of the colours you see – are they warm or cool, do they harmonize subtly or does a contrast catch your eye?

Some colour sense is purely instinctive, some depends on our experience. Just by observing the colours around us, we can turn the world into a source of inspiration.

Primary colours cannot be mixed from any colour base, while all other colours are derived from them.

combining
COLOURS

When using colour, some combinations are more successful than others. Picking the right hues and making sure they work well together are an essential part of good design.

The human eye can see over ten million colours and many of these can be reproduced using either natural or synthetic pigments.

Colour is a major element in the style and atmosphere of your home and, by selecting and combining colours, you can achieve many different effects. Rather than being used in their pure form or on their own, colours are usually mixed with each other to create new colours, and combined into colour schemes.

TONE AND SHADE

There are several ways to look at colours. A colour, or hue, can be primary, secondary or tertiary (two secondary colours mixed). It can be more or less strong: this intensity of colour is called a 'shade'. A colour can be lightened with white (it then becomes a 'tint'), or darkened with black (this is called a 'tone').

Tone is particularly important in design and decoration. Successful design often depends on combining dominant colours that have the same tonal value, and adding accents that are different in tone. This means that instead of ending up with a jumble of colours, you can create a harmonious design.

COLOUR EFFECTS

Colours are also perceived as warm or cool. Warm colours – yellows, reds, pinks, oranges and terracotta colours – seem to come towards you. Use them to make larger spaces seem smaller and to give objects an intimate appeal. Cool colours – the

greens, blues and violets – have the effect of leading the eye into the distance. Use them to lend elegance to your designs and in decoration to make rooms look larger.

COLOUR HARMONIES

Colours can also be combined as harmonies. Harmonious colours, such as a terracotta and a warm yellow, tend to work well together. Designs based on these colours are restful and easy on the eye, but you may need to add a little interest.

Try using different shades of a colour, some lighter, some darker. Or you could add a primary colour accent. This way, you can create designs for anything from painted furniture to needlepoint and still have harmony without blandness.

COLOUR CONTRASTS

Complementary colours – those that sit on opposite sides of the colour wheel – and primary colours are often used to create strong, contrasting colour schemes. Use them

This violet flower is in strong contrast to its yellow background.

to lend drama to designs by placing a red next to a green or using yellow with violet, for instance. You need to be careful with such combinations, however. A lot of red and green may look great at Christmas, but strange the rest of the year!

Use cool colours with warm ones, light colours against dark ones. White is a good accent to use with contrasting colours. Designs usually work best when contrasting colours are used in careful proportions.

NEUTRAL COLOURS

Another effective combination uses the neutral colours of nature. Neutral colours are made up of a little colour mixed in with some black and a lot of white. Think of seashells and sand, or stones and pebbles – and create a design that is a mix of these beige and grey-yellow neutral colours. Accent the design with a stronger colour as a finishing touch.

colour EFFECTS

You can use colour to make a room look larger or more intimate, to heighten or lower the appearance of a ceiling and to create atmosphere.

The reason for being attracted to a particular colour scheme is largely personal – a matter of taste – but that doesn't mean it is the most appropriate scheme for a room. The room may be better suited to another colour because it is on the cold side of the house or the proportions of the room aren't suitable for certain colours.

For the same reasons, a colour scheme seen in a magazine may look very appealing, but when applied in your own home it somehow doesn't work, it doesn't create the mood you want and isn't as stylish as you envisaged. So how do you get it right? You need to consider the size of the room, whether it's light and airy, and what special atmosphere you want to give it.

COLOUR AND SIZE

Lighter colours make a room look bigger while darker ones do the opposite. Then too, cooler shades tend to recede and warmer colours come closer. It's all to do with the way the eye sees and relates to colour. If you look at a landscape, you'll notice how faraway hills and mountains fade into purple, violet and blue even though they are green close up. The closer aspects of the scene appear much warmer with earthy browns and shades of red.

Bear this in mind when planning any colour scheme. Of course, it's not quite that simple. For example, you want to give a large room with a high ceiling a cosy, more intimate look so you need to use dark or strong colours, but do you go for cool or warm shades? Generally, if the room is on the cold, and usually darker, side of the house, choose a warm colour. On the warmer side of the house, you have more leeway to indulge your personal preferences.

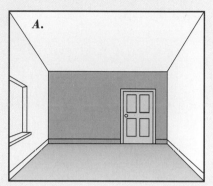

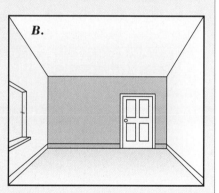

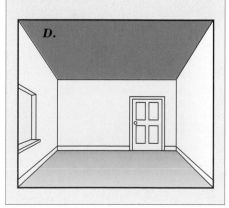

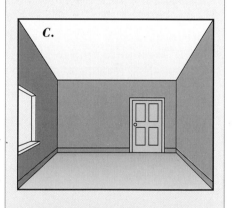

A strong, warm colour (A) makes the wall look closer than a cool colour (B). Use a light colour on the ceiling to make it look higher (C). To make it appear lower and more intimate, use a darker, warm colour (D).

A.

B.

C.

D.

OPTICAL EFFECTS

You may also want to use colour to change certain aspects of a room. If, say, you have a long hallway and you want to make it appear less so, paint the long walls in a pale colour and make the short, end wall a strong dark colour. A warm colour will be even more effective although this may not necessarily suit the overall colour scheme, in which case you must compromise.

Ceilings, too, can be heightened or lowered with the right colours. Use warm, dark colours to bring it down and cool, light colours to lift it. This doesn't mean that the colour must be different to the rest of the room – simply use a lighter or darker shade than on the walls.

A low ceiling can also be given a cornice if it doesn't have one, which is then painted in a darker shade than the ceiling, to give it more height. High ceilings, painted in a strong colour, will appear even lower if you have a border on the walls at waist level. Paint the area below the border a darker shade than that used above the border.

The strong colour on the ceiling makes it appear to be lower.

Small rooms tend to be awkward as we usually want to make them look as spacious as possible. Paint the room in a single light colour with a paler shade on the ceiling if necessary. If the furnishings are the same colour, the scheme will be even more successful.

This doesn't limit you if you want a colourful room. Use accent colour to give warmth and atmosphere to a monochromatic scheme. Use strong contrasting colours for a very stylish look. This can be achieved with bright scatter cushions, a strongly coloured braid or trim added to curtains, an eyecatching vase, rug or wall hanging.

Follow the guidelines and any room can be made to look smart and stylish. Plan the scheme, bearing in mind that the smaller the house or apartment the less colour you should use generally. Then, too, consider what time of day the room is used most and what sort of mood you want to give it.

mixing
PLAIN &
PATTERN

Whether used as dominant elements or as accents, plain and pattern can be mixed and matched to set the style of your designs.

The overall effect of any design is influenced by more than just colour. Another essential element is the balance between the use of pattern and plain textures.

A pattern is the arrangement of a design on a surface. It may appear regular, as in stripes and checks for example, or seem random, as in some florals. A pattern does not need to be fixed. A collection of similar objects can be arranged as a pattern – think of chess pieces on a chessboard, or of serried ranks of toy soldiers on a shelf. Plain is, of course, the opposite, a surface without a design. This does not mean that the surface is without interest – plain surfaces can be textured in many ways.

SUCCESSFUL COMBINATIONS

Patterns can be combined with each other, and are often set against plain. The motifs are infinitely varied, from chintz to ethnic, as are the sizes in which they come.

When combining pattern and plain, there are several options. Pattern can be used as the dominant characteristic, for example as an embroidered motif on a plain background, or in a patchwork quilt where patterned fabrics show up clearly if they are arranged in contrast to plain pieces. In a room, you can use pattern on curtains and upholstery with plain walls, thus pulling the look together.

Pattern can also be used as an accent to liven up and lend character to an otherwise plain surface: as a stencilled motif on a chest of drawers, on cushions in a room decorated in plain colours, or as edging on a pair of simple curtains.

RANGE OF PATTERNS

Patterns vary in scale and come in a wide variety of shapes, from traditional soft coloured florals to monochrome contemporary geometrics.

Floral designs range from large overall patterns to delicate cottage sprigs. If you are combining patterns for a quilted patchwork, for example, bear in mind that small designs often work best. You might have to cut up a large design which will reduce its impact.

If decorating a large room, think of your colour scheme as a family: use a large design on the curtains –

the parents – and a smaller coordinating design for cushions – the children. A combination of small designs can be very effective when used in smaller rooms.

Geometrics make a bold statement – concentrate on one focal element and coordinate it with a plain colour. Check and stripe designs can similarly be coordinated with a wide range of patterns.

USING PLAIN AND PATTERN

Mixing plains with patterns highlights the colours used in the design. The effect also depends on the background colour – the same design may blend well with

The strong, modern lines of these geometric patterns are beautifully set off by the plain white wall.

a toning background, and look totally different against a contrasting background that highlights details of the pattern.

To work out how to use patterns and plains together, decide what style and colours you would like to have. Look for a pattern that reflects the mood you want to evoke – it could be romantic flowers, a strong ethnic feel or modern simplicity. Use this as the focal point, and then find plain colours to coordinate.

COMBINING PATTERNS

The secret of using patterns together is to choose elements that are in harmony with each other – for example, light stripes and small naive checks can go well together, especially if the colours tone in.

You can see good examples of coordinated ranges of fabrics and paints in the shops and in the catalogues of many companies.

chapter two

THE
HALL

The Hall

CONTENTS

embossed patterns

Instead of the traditional light stippling of paint, a mixture of gesso powder and water is used with a stencil to create a raised pattern. When dry, it can be painted to match the background or in another colour.

You will need

MATT WHITE EMULSION PAINT

PAINTBRUSH

PENCIL AND RULER

MEASURING TAPE

STENCIL

MASKING TAPE

GESSO POWDER

REPOSITIONAL SPRAY-ON ADHESIVE

MEDIUM AND FINE GRADE SANDPAPER

CRAFT KNIFE OR SCALPEL

MIXING BOWL

PAINT, FOR FINAL COAT

Although an ordinary stencil has been used for this simple technique, the end result is very different from the traditional coloured pattern created with paint.

The raised effect is made with a mixture of water and gesso. Gesso is a plaster-like powder that is much finer than the cellulose filler used to make walls good and is available from decorating stores and arts and craft shops. Unlike the usual technique of stencilling with paint, the gesso is worked without the addition of colour and dries white, like plaster. Once dry, it can be painted and decorated as required.

USE EMBOSSED STENCILS ON • walls • friezes • dados • boxes • lamp bases picture frames • chests.

17

The preparation for using gesso is the same as traditional stencilling. Make good the surface and measure and mark the pattern or border. There's no need to mask parts of the stencil – the whole pattern is used, so choose a suitable motif (patterns created by overlapping stencils aren't suitable). Secure the stencil to the background with spray-on adhesive and begin to work the gesso as shown. If you want to use colour, add paint or inks when you make up the gesso or simply paint over the gesso when it is dry.

GESSO

Gesso has been used for centuries to provide a smooth surface for painting. Murals and frescoes created on a surface made from glue and gesso date as far back as the Middle Ages and the Rennaisance. Today, gesso is used for restoration work and for casting and repairing mouldings. Artists still use it for certain specialist techniques such as tempera, which involves paints created with egg yolk and different colour pigments.
Gesso is available in its original powder form as well as ready mixed (acrylic gesso comes in tins and has a fairly thick consistency). Gesso powder is used here as it is easier to control the consistency by mixing it with a little water.

1 Prime the surface to be decorated by applying a thin undercoat of matt white emulsion paint. This will improve the absorbency of the gesso and make working easier.

2 To create a border, measure the width that you require, using the stencil as a guide. Make stencil repeat marks along the border. Leave at least 6mm / ¼in between repeats.

3 To add some texture to the background (this is optional), cover the area inside the marked border area with masking tape. Tape both sides of the border along its whole length.

4 Mix the gesso with a little water. The consistency should be that of runny yogurt. If you want to colour the gesso rather than painting it later, add the colour now.

5 Apply the gesso to the surface excluding the masked border. Use thick, bold brush strokes to leave a textured finish. Leave to dry completely before you begin working with the stencil.

*Crafty*tip

In order not to damage the wet embossed stencil, work alternate squares with gesso and then leave them to dry completely before stencilling the remaining squares.

6 Remove the masking tape strips from inside the border area by lifting and peeling them away gently. Do this very carefully so as not to damage the outline of the textured border.

The fleur-de-lys makes an excellent motif for this technique. It is particularly useful to camouflage uneven walls. The background can be textured but this is optional. Paint the wall and then highlight the pattern.

SAFETY FIRST
Make sure that you always wear a protective face mask and that you work in a well-ventilated room when you are working with the spray-on adhesive. Direct inhalation of the fumes could be dangerous.

7 Lightly spray the back of the stencil with some adhesive and place it in one of the previously marked squares. Apply the water and gesso mixture as thickly as possible, using a small paintbrush. Gently pull away the stencil and leave the gesso to dry.

8 Work alternate squares in this way, along the length of the border. Leave the gesso to dry before filling in the remaining squares. When dry, sand the raised patterns ever so lightly to smooth and level them so that they are all about the same height.

9 Using a craft knife or a scalpel, work round the edges of the embossed motif with the blade to tidy up and smooth the edges. Use the knife to remove any unwanted pieces of gesso that may detract from the overall appearance.

10 In a mixing bowl, make up a solution of one part PVA glue diluted with two parts water. Mix the two together well until they are completely blended.

11 Using a wide paintbrush, apply the glue solution over the raised stencil pattern in order to seal and strengthen it. Leave the glue solution until completely dry.

12 Paint the stencilled surface as required. You can use emulsion paint, which is easy to apply and dries quickly, as well as using oil and watercolour paints.

final touch

Instead of painting the whole of the stencilled surface in a single colour, apply a base coat all over. Then highlight the embossed pattern with either a lighter or darker shade. If you prefer, you can use a different colour to complement or contrast with the base coat.

Motifs, such as leaves, can be used to create a random pattern. Paint them mid-green and then highlight them in a lighter shade.

dried *flower* MIRROR

Use a combination of air-dried flowers and glycerine-preserved foliage to add a decorative edging to a mirror which acts as a frame.

This oval mirror has no frame apart from that provided by the dried flowers. It is a piece of mirror glass, cut to shape, to which a floral decoration is applied with a hot-glue gun.

A mirror decorated in this way looks spectacular in a hall or over a dressing table in the bedroom. It does not have to be oval – the idea works just as well in the round, or on a square or rectangular mirror.

Although the design goes all round the mirror, try and create a focal point where the design is built up more than in other areas, usually to the bottom left or right, and off-centre.

Avoid using too many colours as this will create a garish effect. Go for subtle combinations in the same tones. Here shades of pink and cream predominate with the peonies providing the mainstay of the decoration.

decorating the mirror

When having the mirror glass cut, ask for holes to be drilled in it so you can hang the mirror. The mirror shown is 46cm / 18in long and 36cm / 14in wide. Clean the mirror before you apply the dried flower edging.

1 Tie a knot at one end of a length of cord and pass the other end through a hole in the mirror (A). Pass the cord along the back and out to the front through the other hole. Knot the end.

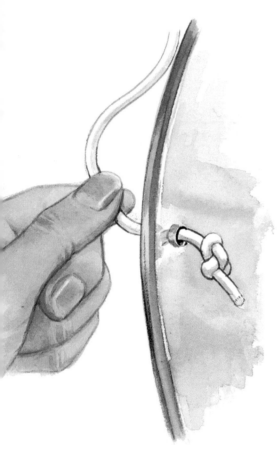

A. Trap the knotted end of the cord at the front and pass the other end along the back.

2 Using a hot-glue gun, attach the glycerine-preserved copper beech in a complete circle all around the mirror, overlapping the leaves slightly.

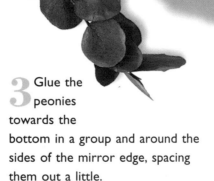

3 Glue the peonies towards the bottom in a group and around the sides of the mirror edge, spacing them out a little.

4 Add in the cedar roses in groups between the peonies and interspersed amongst the main group at the base of the mirror.

5 Form small bunches of wheat with short stems (don't wire them as this will add too much bulk), and add them at intervals around the design, so that the spikes of the wheat overlap the outer edges of the mirror, as well as protruding into the centre, breaking up the predominantly round edge of the design.

VARIATIONS

HYDRANGEAS – these are as spectacular as peonies and come in different colours. For a blue display, combine them with smaller flowers such as larkspur and use cornflowers to fill in the gaps. Lavender is also suitable.

ROSES – choose dried yellow roses and set them off with Chinese lanterns, canary grass, yellow helichrysum and tansy, sunray or achillea for the smaller flowers.

6 Add in smaller items, using the colours to dictate the position – cream helichrysum is used here to highlight the design and the deep pink, dyed gypsophila adds colour contrast to the edging.

Ready-made eyelets and cord (left) or clip-on hooks (below) are used to secure curtain to rail.

no-sew CURTAINS

Draped to please and not a stitch in sight, these curtains are finished with self-adhesive hemming and clip-on hooks or ready-made eyelets.

You will need

CURTAIN FABRIC

IRONING BOARD AND IRON

CLEAN TEA TOWEL

BUMPER PACK OF SELF-ADHESIVE HEMMING

FABRIC SCISSORS

TIEBACK

FOR THE PATTERNED CURTAIN:

READY-MADE EYELETS, 3M / 10FT CORD, TASSEL TRIM AND FABRIC GLUE

FOR THE SHEER CURTAIN:

CLIP-ON CURTAIN HOOKS

Give your windows a new dress-ing with these easy-to-make curtains. Choose your fabric according to the finished effect you want. A heavy, patterned furnishing fabric gives a more formal appearance, while a lightweight sheer fabric, such as voile, produces a light sum-mery look. The patterned curtain is made with 120cm / 48in-wide fabric and is hung using ready-made eye-lets. A tassel trim is fixed using fab-ric glue. The voile curtain is made with 150cm / 60in-wide fabric and is hung with clip-on hooks. Both of the fabric widths are suitable for win-dows up to 90cm / 36in wide. For wider windows, up to 180cm / 72in, make two curtains and drape one length to each side.

HOW MUCH FABRIC?

Measure from the curtain rail to the floor. Add on 50cm / 20in if using sheer fabric or 1m / 40in if using fur-nishing fabric (you will also need this length of tassel trim), to allow the curtain to drape on the floor.

23

making the curtains

*Choose a sheer voile or
furnishing fabric but avoid
velvet or any fabric with a
pile. They are not suitable
for this type of curtain.*

**A. Fix the self-adhesive hemming
by pressing. Place a damp cloth on
the fold and use a dry-heat setting.**

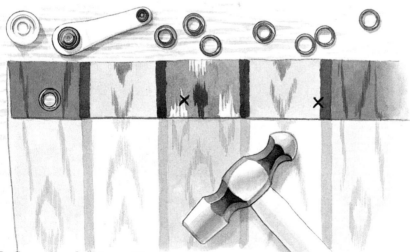

B. Secure eyelets in position.

**C. To hang the
curtain, thread
the cord
through each
eyelet and
around the
pole. Knot cord
ends to secure.**

Making the hems

1 Place the fabric right side down on to an ironing board and fold over a 2.5cm / 1in hem along the selvedge. Press with an iron.

2 Insert the self-adhesive hemming (A) and fuse together according to the instructions on the pack. Repeat with the second selvedge.

3 Check that the top and bottom edges of the fabric are straight and trim if necessary. Turn over and seal the edges as for the selvedges.

Using sheer fabric

1 Attach the clip-on hooks about 15cm / 6in apart.

2 Hang the curtain and drape to one side with a tieback.

*Choose the tassel trim and the
cord to complement the colour of
the curtain fabric.*

Using patterned fabric

1 Lay out the tassel trim on to the right-hand side of the fabric and attach it using the fabric glue. Leave for about 30 minutes to dry thoroughly. Turn under the raw edge of the tassel trim and secure in place with the fabric glue.

2 To insert the eyelets, place the top edge of the fabric right side down on a clean, flat surface.

3 Place the eyelet rings on to the fabric about 13cm / 5in apart. Mark a cross 1.5cm / ½in down from the top edge, for each eyelet.

4 Secure the eyelets in position according to the instructions on the pack (B).

5 Insert the cord through eyelets and over the pole (C), and drape the curtain with a tieback.

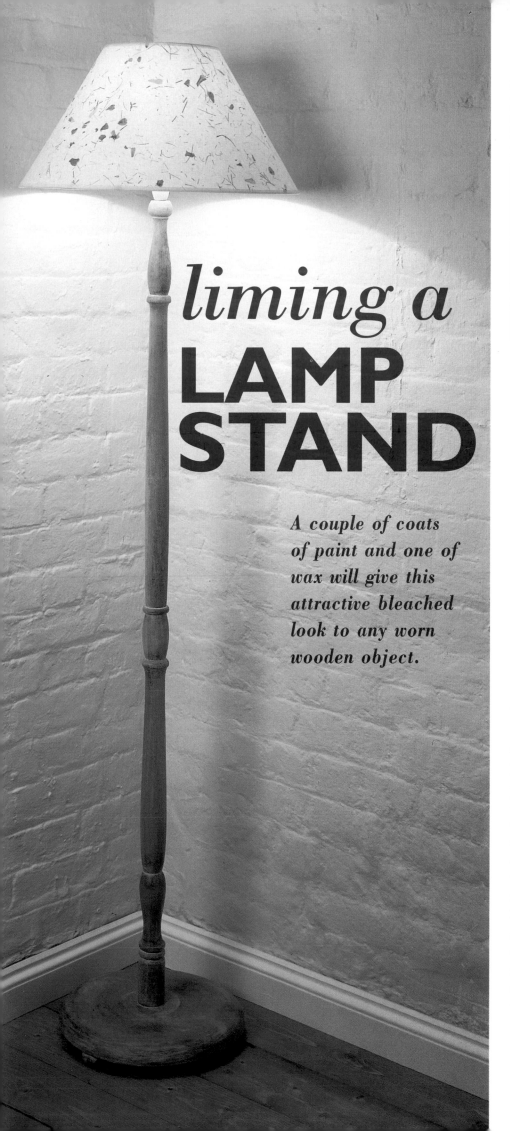

liming a LAMP STAND

A couple of coats of paint and one of wax will give this attractive bleached look to any worn wooden object.

You will need

HOT-AIR GUN OR LIQUID PAINT STRIPPER

OLD LAMP STAND

SCRAPER

SANDPAPER

GREEN WATER-BASED WOOD STAIN

PAINTBRUSHES

LIMING WAX

FINE STEEL WOOL

WAX FURNITURE POLISH

This makeover uses the liming paint technique (see Chapter Five, Limed Wood, pp109–10). Although an old lamp stand was used here, you can apply this technique to any old or worn household items, such as chairs, sideboards and cupboards. Liming wax (available from decorating shops, paint shops and some arts and crafts shops) works best on open-grained wood, so choose an object made of a relatively robust wood, such as oak, which lends itself to this attractive bleached look.

STRIP AND SAND

Whatever the object, it is important to strip it down completely before starting. Different effects can be achieved according to whether the paint is removed using a hot-air gun or liquid paint stripper (see overleaf). After sanding, the wood is stained with a water-based wood stain (green is used here, but use a colour of your choice). Two or even three coats of stain can be applied according to the shade you want. Liming wax is then applied, using a soft cloth; the wax highlights the contours of the wood grain. The final finish is achieved by applying a coat of wax furniture polish, which gives the stand a soft sheen.

liming the lamp stand

Stripping the lamp stand with a hot-air gun will make the paint bubble and burn. This will affect the colour of the wood, creating a mottled effect. If you don't have a hot-air gun, remove the paint or varnish with a liquid stripper.

1 Strip the old paint from the lamp stand using a hot-air gun. This will cause the paint to bubble, making it easier to remove.

A. Sand the lamp stand down, using medium grade sandpaper.

2 Scrape off the layers of paint and sand the stand down, following the grain, to remove any stubborn bits of paint (A). Wipe the stand clean to remove any flakes of paint.

3 Colour the stand green using wood stain. Apply the stain with a paintbrush and wipe off any excess with a cloth (B). Apply one coat. For a stronger colour, apply two coats of stain. Leave to dry.

4 Apply the liming wax, working along the grain (C). Leave for 10 minutes.

B. Apply the green stain with the paintbrush, then wipe off excess with a cloth and leave to dry.

5 Wipe off the excess liming wax and polish the stand with furniture polish. Use polish in a tin rather than the spray-on variety.

SAFETY FIRST

Take care when using liquid paint stripper and always wear rubber gloves. If using a hot-air gun, don't leave it unattended while burning.

Craftytip

Instead of wood stain, use an emulsion paint diluted with water.

C. Apply the liming wax with a piece of steel wool, taking off the excess with a rag.

painting on glass

With a little practice you can create stunning and colourful effects on glass using specially formulated paints.

It's possible to achieve quite painterly effects, with subtle blends of colours, when painting glass. Draw out your design with a relief outliner then work within these lines to add colour to your piece. Practise using the relief outliner so that you get clean lines without blobs or fuzziness.

Blending colours within one designated area can be done in one of two ways. You can apply colours over a wash of clear glass paint, working while the wash is still wet. You can also tint this clear paint to provide a very light base colour, which can be painted over.

For stronger definition of two or more colours within an area, without separating areas with relief outliner, mix coloured and clear paints in equal parts. Paint in the first area then add the second colour – the colours will blend slightly at the edges, creating a very natural look without a hard line.

Finally, the relief outliner in metallic shades can be used to add soft definition to a design when the paint has dried completely. It will pick up the light and can be used to add texture and to highlight areas. USE GLASS PAINTS • on transparent items such as candle holders • on window panes and glass door panels • on clear bottles • on mirrors.

If working on a curved surface, such as a vase, you may find that cutting the design into sections makes it easier to fit around the inside curve.

Craftytip

Hold the relief outliner like a pen, using your thumb and forefinger to apply pressure. Squeeze until the outliner just begins to come out, then apply the nozzle at an angle of about 45 degrees.

1 Wash the article being decorated in warm soapy water, then wipe over with white spirit to remove any grease, which will prevent the paint from adhering to the glass.

2 Measure the area to be decorated and enlarge the design to size. Position the design under the glass and secure with masking tape.

3 Trace the design using black relief outliner, being aware that the depth of the glass will appear to distort the lines. Work down and across from the top, so you don't smudge lines already in place. Leave any long straight lines.

4 Wipe the tip of the nozzle regularly to prevent blobs from forming. Leave the design in a warm place for about two hours until it is dry.

5 When dry, fill in any long straight lines, such as frame lines. It's worth doing all of these in one go so that they look fluid rather than jerky or disjointed.

6 To blend colours, apply a wash of clear varnish as a base coat over the area to be blended. Clean the brush with white spirit between colours (a touch of green paint is added to the varnish here to make it visible).

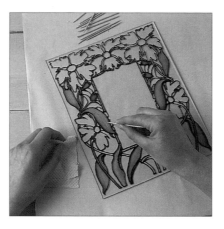

7 Working quickly before the varnish dries, brush stripes of two or more colours into the varnish. With smooth flowing brushstrokes, blend the colours into one another at the point where they meet.

8 Add details with scratch work. Leave the paint to set for 10-15 minutes, then while the paint is still tacky, scribe lines with a cocktail stick. Clean the stick with a piece of kitchen paper after each line.

9 To slow down the drying time of the varnish, mix equal parts of paint and varnish. Do this with a pipette for accuracy, using an ice-cube tray as a palette. This gives you more time to work without visible strokes forming. Use a cocktail stick rather than a paintbrush to mix the paint to avoid bubbles forming.

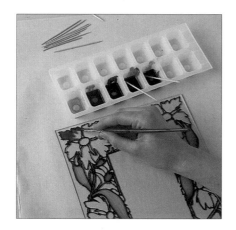

10 To keep two colours separate and to prevent them from blending in one area, blend the colours as above with varnish. Working quickly, paint the first colour, leaving a space for the second. Apply the paint liberally for a jewel-like quality.

11 Apply the second colour while the first is still wet. If necesary, turn the item as you work so that each brushstroke flows easily.

12 Complete the painting, using colours straight from the pot to fill in details such as flower centres. Leave to dry in a dust-free area for at least 24 hours.

13 Using a gold relief outliner, define the contour lines and add details to the paintwork as required. Leave for at least two hours to dry.

final touch

When completely dry, clean both sides of the glass with a little white spirit. To use the glass as a frame, mount it on a backing board with clip-on fasteners.

You can add colour and interest to enhance textured papers with two shades of paint.

paint effects on textured paper

You will need

EMULSION PAINT IN TWO SHADES

TWO PAINTBRUSHES

OLD SAUCERS, PLATES OR DISHES FOR THE PAINT

Woodchip wallpaper, used to disguise uneven walls in many older homes, has rather a bad name among decorators, but as it is quite difficult to remove and often means walls have to be replastered, it usually stays in place. One way of disguising it, or even enhancing it, is to use a paint effect.

Textured wallpapers also take paint effects well. Paint on one colour, working it evenly into the surface. Then choose another colour to dry brush on to the surface – looking at some of the effects overleaf to get an idea of how toning and contrasting shades work.

If you want a subtle effect on your walls, choose toning colours, that is those in a related shade. Contrasting colours produce a more dramatic effect, as does gold, which probably works best over a deep shade, such as red or blue, in a dark hallway. It also works in areas used mainly in the evening, which you are likely to light with lamps or candles. If you do choose gold, beware – from certain angles it can look dark brown or black.

USE THIS PAINT EFFECT • on textured wallpaper • to enhance woodchip wallpaper.

*W*hen applying the second colour to the textured surface, you need to use a fairly dry brush so that you can work the raised areas only, leaving the background colour to show through for a mottled finish.

Crafty tip

Apply the finish to a small section and check the result before doing a whole wall.

1 Apply the base coat emulsion (dark green is used here) to the textured paper, using a brush to work it well into the nooks and crannies of the paper. Leave to dry.

2 Dip a dry brush into the second shade of emulsion (mid-green), just to coat the ends of the bristles. Work the brush on a clean saucer or plate so that the bristles are lightly coated.

3 Brush the paint lightly on to the textured paper. Do this with a very light touch so that only the raised areas take up the colour and try to keep the effect even.

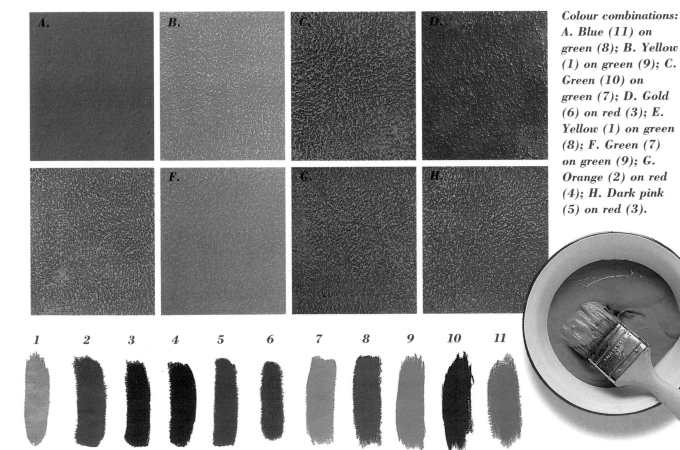

Colour combinations: A. Blue (11) on green (8); B. Yellow (1) on green (9); C. Green (10) on green (7); D. Gold (6) on red (3); E. Yellow (1) on green (8); F. Green (7) on green (9); G. Orange (2) on red (4); H. Dark pink (5) on red (3).

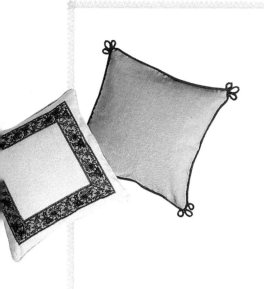

chapter three

THE LIVING ROOM

CONTENTS

trimming cushions

Give your cushions a new look by trimming them with cord and braid or even shells. Similar cushions cost a small fortune in the shops, but you can do it for a fraction of the cost.

Buy untrimmed cushions from department stores or start with ones you already have. Let your room's colour scheme dictate your choice of trimmings and cushion fabric. Dress up plainer fabrics with ornate braids and cords. For rich fabrics, such as kelim (traditionally woven Middle Eastern rugs) and velvet, use more unusual trimmings such as shells to decorate the cushion.

USE TRIMMING ON • cushions • tiebacks • plain curtains.

You will need

TAPE MEASURE

PINS AND NEEDLES

ADHESIVE TAPE

CUSHION PADS AND COVERS

SCISSORS

MATCHING THREADS

FOR THE KELIM CUSHION

READY-MADE KELIM CUSHION

FINE NEEDLE WITH LARGE EYE

1 CARD OF SILK THREAD PER 20 BEADS AND SHELLS

7 BEADS PER 10CM / 4IN

7 PIERCED SHELLS PER 10CM / 4IN

FOR THE CORD CUSHION

CORD

LENGTH: OUTER EDGE + 122CM / 4FT

FOR THE BRAIDED CUSHION

BRAID

LENGTH: 4 X ONE SIDE OF CUSHION

FOR THE RAFFIA FRINGE CUSHION

RAFFIA FRINGE

TISSUE PAPER

PIPING CORD

You can either use existing cushion covers or buy ready-made ones to decorate with a variety of trimmings, such as cord, braid and raffia fringing. The pierced shells are available from bead and shell shops.

LOOPED CORD

1 To prevent the cord untwisting, wrap a piece of adhesive tape around both ends. Unpick a small section of the seam at the cushion corner and poke one end of the cord into it. Pin the cord neatly around the cushion sides, creating three loops at each corner, with the middle loop lying centrally over each corner. Make sure that the cord stays tightly twisted.

2 To attach the cord to the cushion, slip-stitch (see below left) it to the cushion with matching thread. The loops need to be sewn together where they cross over as well as to the cushion fabric. Finish off at the point where you started and poke the remaining cord end into the hole. Sew up the hole with a few neat stitches.

KELIM AND SHELLS

1 Bend the top of the kelim side of the cushion over and push the needle and silk thread up through the kelim, 2.5cm / 1in down from the seam. Pull the needle out at the join between the backing fabric and the kelim. Release the bent-over kelim and the end of the thread should disappear. Secure the thread with small stitches where the two fabrics join. Thread a bead on to the end.

2 Thread the needle through the back of the shell and then through again. Wind the silk thread around the thread in between the bead and the shell about four times, keeping it fairly loose. Then push the thread down through the bead. Sew a couple of holding stitches and repeat the process of sewing through the kelim to hide the end of the thread.

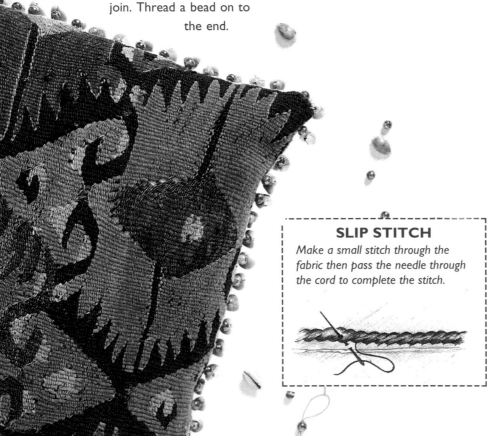

SLIP STITCH
Make a small stitch through the fabric then pass the needle through the cord to complete the stitch.

WORK BOX

CORDS

Cords are available in different widths ranging from 5mm / ⅕in to 15mm / ⅔in. The smaller size can be used for creating loops but the larger cord is too thick for small items like cushions. Flanged cord has a fabric flap that allows you to sew it directly into a seam if you are making cushion covers from scratch.

Trimmed cushions give an original and elegant touch to your home decoration.

MITRED BRAID

1 Lay the cushion on a flat surface and cut four pieces of braid slightly shorter than the cushion width. Position each braid length 4cm / 1½in from the edge and pin and tack in place. Make sure that any design faces the same way. Hem-stitch along the edges leaving the corner areas free. Fold the corners under at a 45° angle and press with a cool iron.

2 For each corner, join the mitres together at just the inner and outer corners, with a few hem stitches. Then cut off the free ends so that they are hidden when folded underneath. Join the mitres together with small stitches in matching thread then sew the braid edges to the cushion fabric itself, in hem stitch. Press with a cool iron.

HEM STITCH

Come up through the braid and pick up a small stitch in the fabric. Then push the needle diagonally up through the back of the braid.

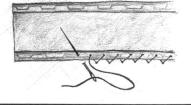

RAFFIA FRINGE

1 Starting and finishing at one corner, hand sew the raffia fringe behind the cushion piping. Take a piece of tissue paper the size and colour of your cushion and sketch a design for the cord. Begin and end the design with a swirl to hide the cord ends.

2 Pin the tissue paper to the front of the cushion and tack along the design in a contrasting thread. Rip off the paper leaving the stitches in place and sew the cord over the tacking stitches. When you have finished, pull out all the tacks.

pretty
SHEER

Made with a self frill at the top, these unlined curtains drape softly over the window without restricting too much light.

Unlined curtains look lovely made up in sheer fabrics for use at a window where you want full curtains without restricting the light from coming in. They will not give you privacy at night, however, when your lights are switched on. You may need a plain blind behind them, to pull down when it gets dark.

Use a regular or pinch-pleat heading tape and for extra effect, fold the fabric over at the top to form a self frill. Hang the curtains from a pole or an ordinary rail.

To make a self frill, allow an extra 25cm / 10in length when cutting the fabric. Increase or decrease this amount according to the length of the actual curtain. As a guide, the self frill shouldn't be more than about one- fifth of the overall length of the curtain. If in doubt, fold one end of the fabric over the length required to see what it looks like.

You will need

SHEER FABRIC, SUCH AS MUSLIN, AND MATCHING THREAD

SCISSORS

TAPE MEASURE

HEADING TAPE

SEWING MACHINE

IRON

SATIN BIAS BINDING, TWICE THE LENGTH PLUS TWICE THE WIDTH OF THE CURTAINS

making sheer curtains

The satin bias binding is used to edge the two inside edges of the curtains (where they meet) as well as the self frill. The bottom hem of the curtain is sewn by hand but, if you wish, you can trim this with bias binding as well.

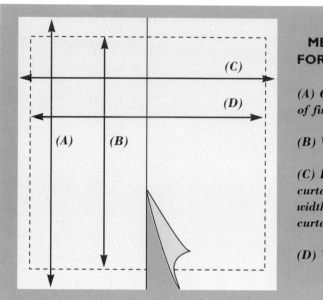

MEASURING FOR CURTAINS

(A) Overall length of finished curtain.

(B) Window height.

(C) Length of curtain track and width of gathered curtain.

(D) Window width.

1 Measure and cut fabric to size, allowing 25cm / 10in for the self frill plus a hem allowance. Join the widths using a flat fell or French seam (see Chapter Four, Unlined Curtains, pp63-66).

2 Fold the bias binding in half lengthways and bind the top edge, sandwiching the raw edges in the fold. Machine stitch in place.

3 On the outside edge of the curtain, make a narrow double hem. If the fabric has a simple selvedge, you may be able to leave it unhemmed.

4 Turn 25cm / 10in of the fabric to the right side at the bound top edge of the curtain. Press the top fold.

5 Bind the inner, central edge of the curtain (where the pair meet) using satin bias binding as in

Step 2, and binding the side edge of the overlapped top (the self frill) in with the curtain.

6 Pin the heading tape to the wrong side at the top of the curtain. Stitch through all thicknesses at the top and bottom of the heading tape.

7 Draw up the heading tape to the length of the track, tack the hem and hang the curtains. Leave them to drop before hand sewing the hem in place.

Crafty tip

Before cutting sheer fabrics such as voile or muslin to length, they should be washed as some of these fabrics may well shrink.

Using bias binding, trim the top frill with a contrasting colour to match other fabrics or furnishings in the room. This could be plain or patterned (you can make your own bias strips from narrow widths of fabric cut on the cross grain and joined).

Using ribbon, edge the top frill with a toning or contrasting colour as above. You can also use ribbon to bind the central edge. Ribbon-threaded lace can be used in the same way.

ruched
PELMET

If your fabric has a design with an interesting shape, use the outline to create the decorative lower edge of the pelmet, and add a padded, ruched border to the top.

The design of the fabric has been allowed to dictate the shape of the pelmet, which is quite deep. This is particularly suitable for a tall window with a sweep of floor-length curtains to keep the proportions correct. For smaller windows or where curtains only fall to the windowsill, especially in rooms with low ceilings, don't make the pelmet too deep, and keep the outline simple.

The pelmet is made more imposing by the addition of a ruched top. This is made by sewing a tube of fabric to twice the length of the pelmet and stuffing it with wadding before ruching the fabric evenly over the top.

Use a touch-and-close fastener to attach the pelmet to a batten over the window, ensuring that the pelmet goes around the edges to the wall to provide a neat finish.

You will need

PIECE OF FABRIC TO THE LENGTH OF THE BATTEN ABOVE THE WINDOW PLUS TWICE THE DEPTH OF THE BATTEN BY TWICE THE DROP OF THE PELMET, PLUS 5CM / 2IN SEAM ALLOWANCES

DOUBLE-SIDED ADHESIVE PELMET CARD

SCISSORS

MATCHING THREAD

SEWING MACHINE

FABRIC FOR RUCHED TUBE

DOUBLE STRIP OF SELF-ADHESIVE TOUCH-AND-CLOSE FASTENER, TO LENGTH PLUS TWICE THE DEPTH OF THE BATTEN

WADDING TO THE LENGTH OF THE PELMET BY 15CM / 6IN

SAFETY PIN

making the ruched pelmet

*If cutting a pelmet to the shape of the fabric pattern,
allow for matching and centring the pattern. Calculate
the fabric required according to the length and depth of
the batten above the window, and to the design required
for the pelmet.*

Craftytip

A decorative pelmet such as
this works best with toning
curtains in a plain colour. If
you use the same fabric for
the curtains, the effect is lost.

*C. Use a safety
pin to pull the
wadding through
the fabric tube.*

1 Look at the fabric design and see
if it suggests a shape for the
pelmet. In this case, the design
suggested round and pointed scallops.
Cut out the fabric (which becomes
the lining) to the required width and
depth of the finished pelmet,
following the shape of the design.

*A. Transfer the
fabric outline on to
the pelmet card.*

2 Lay out the pelmet card,
squared side facing. Place the
lining fabric on top and draw the
outline on the grid (A). Cut out
the pelmet shape.

3 Place the pelmet card
on the wrong side of
the remaining fabric and
draw round it, being careful to
align the pelmet edges with the
fabric design in the same way as on
the lining fabric.

4 Add on a 2.5cm / 1in seam
allowance all round and cut out
the fabric for the front of the pelmet.

5 Peel away the backing
from the pelmet card and
attach the larger piece of
fabric to the pelmet card,
positioning it carefully and
smoothing the fabric well.
Clip into the seam allowance
and fold it back to the other
side of the pelmet, removing
the second piece of backing.

6 Apply the lining fabric
to the back of the
pelmet, covering the turned-in
seam allowance (B). Trim to
fit if necessary.

7 Cut a piece of fabric 10cm
/ 4in wide by twice the
length of the pelmet, joining strips
as necessary. With right sides
together, fold in half lengthways
and seam down the side to form
a tube. Turn the tube through.

*B. Line the back of the pelmet
with the fabric you cut first.*

8 Roll the length of wadding in a
'swiss roll' shape and bind it
with thread along its length.

9 Attach a safety pin to one end
of the wadding and thread it
through the tube, spreading the
gathers evenly as you go (C).

10 Slip-stitch the ends of the
tube closed and then
slip-stitch the tube to the top of the
fabric-covered pelmet.

11 Attach a strip of touch-and-
close fastener to the top
inside of the pelmet just
below the ruched top.
Attach the corresponding
hooked strip to the front
and side edges of the batten.

12 Attach the pelmet to the
batten, making sharp folds
where it goes round from the front
to form the side edges.

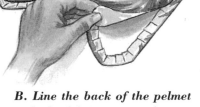

Add an original touch to your curtains with these witty tiebacks – three different looks for three different styles of room.

creating clever
TIEBACKS

Rather than change your curtains, which is an expensive and time-consuming operation, you can liven up your existing drapes with new tiebacks. Go for something unusual to create a strong look as it is more effective when tiebacks are made of a material different from that of the curtains.

With shop-bought tiebacks you tend to have the problem of finding something that matches your existing fabric. Making your own gives you the freedom to experiment with all kinds of novelty materials.

CHOOSING MATERIALS

The three styles shown here are very easy to make – none took longer than a couple of hours.

You can match tieback flowers, foliage and even fruit to the predominant colours in your patterned fabrics. An autumnal display of roses, apples and pears would look good in a living room, dining room or a country-style kitchen. For plain materials, choose a colour or theme that coordinates with the rest of the room.

The teddy bear tieback can be made out of scraps of material left over from the curtains or any other soft furnishings from your children's room.

The starfish tieback will enhance a room which has a seaside theme, whether you have a painting of the sea, or boats, or even a real sea view.

You will need

FOR THE FLOWER TIEBACK

12 LONG STEMMED SILK FLOWERS

4 STRANDS OF FRUIT

FOR THE TEDDY BEAR TIEBACK

SCISSORS

50CM / 19 IN OF TWO CONTRASTING FABRICS

PINS

MATCHING THREADS

SEWING MACHINE

KNITTING NEEDLE

KAPOK WADDING

SEWING NEEDLE

DARK BLUE EMBROIDERY THREAD

FOR THE STARFISH TIEBACK

BUTTON CURTAIN HOLD-BACK KIT

SMALL PIECE OF KAPOK WADDING

STRONG EPOXY GLUE

AN OLD PIECE OF FABRIC

STARFISH

how to make the tiebacks

Coordinate your tiebacks with your decor – choose from flowers and fruit, a starfish for a seaside theme, or bears and rabbits for a child's room.

FLOWERS AND FRUIT THEME

1 Take two flowers. At the stem ends twist loops of about 3cm / 1¼ in diameter (A). Cross the flowers just below the heads and twist together to form a frame of about 85cm / 33 ⅛in .

2 Twist a fruit stem around the frame next to the flowers. Keep wrapping more flowers and foliage hiding the frame (B). Wrap a piece of fruit around the end section by the last rose, hiding the stems.

A. Cross the first two flowers and twist to form the frame.

B. Continue winding flowers and fruit so that they conceal the frame.

SEASIDE THEME

1 Follow the manufacturer's instructions to construct the button tieback, placing a piece of wadding between the button and the fabric to raise it slightly.

2 Glue the covered button and the back of the starfish. Follow the pack instructions and stick one to the other. Leave to dry and attach to wall as per manufacturer's instructions.

FOR THE NURSERY

1 Enlarge the templates to twice the size given (see Enlarging a Design p6). Cut out six bears from one fabric and six rabbits from the other. Pin the two bear shapes together, right sides facing, and sew, allowing for 5mm / ¼in seam and a gap in the leg.

2 Zig zag the raw edges. Cut a V into any sharp corners to finish. Turn the bears the right way out through the gap in the leg and push through the arms and legs with a knitting needle. Iron, stuff with kapok and sew up the opening. Repeat with the other bears and rabbits, embroidering the faces if you wish. Sew together in a chain by their paws. Cut two rectangles 10 x 5cm / 4 x 2in and sew to make two tubes. Turn out, sew to last paws to form loops and hook on to the wall.

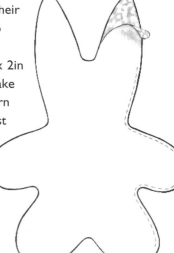

bolster
CUSHION

The shape and tailored appearance of bolster cushions make an attractive addition to a sofa and also provide added comfort.

In Victorian times bolsters were covered in a white embroidered cotton or linen case and used down the centre of beds – a fashion you can revive by increasing the length of the bolster made here. They are also ideal for use at the ends of a sofa.

This type of bolster is covered in a fine cotton and given a tailored appearance, with piping at both ends and decorative tassels where the fabric is drawn in. You can buy covered bolster pads from large department stores, or you can make your own to the size required using lining fabric. Stuff the bolster quite firmly – it is meant to have substance.

The bolster cushion pad is covered with a rectangle of fabric, with a zip set in the seam for easy removal and washing. Tubes of fabric are used to cover the ends, drawn up to provide full gathers, with toning piping set in the seam, and tassels used to disguise the centre of the gathers.

making the bolster cushion

You can make the bolster cushion smaller or larger, as required. If making your own pad, make sure it is stuffed quite firmly.

1 Cut a piece of fabric to the length of the bolster, by its circumference, plus 12mm / ½in seam allowances on each edge (in this case, 61x46cm / 24x18in).

2 With the right sides together, fold the fabric in half and tack the seam. Stitch 6cm / 2¼in at each end of the seam and press open.

3 Centre the zip over the seam, face down, and pin, tack and machine stitch in place, using a zipper foot.

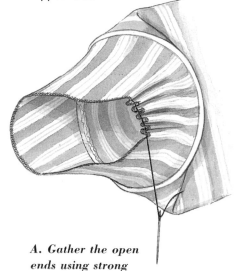

A. Gather the open ends using strong thread.

4 Cover the piping cord with bias binding. Cut two lengths to the circumference of the bolster. With the raw edges together, stitch the covered piping to each end of the cover, using a zipper foot. Join the piping by butting up the ends of the cord and overlapping the bias binding. Clip into the stitched seam to provide ease.

5 Cut two rectangles of fabric for each end of the bolster, with the length the same as the circumference of the bolster and the width equal to the radius (in this case 61x9cm / 24x3½in) plus seam allowances.

6 With the right sides facing, stitch the two ends of each rectangle. Pin one side of the fabric to the circular end of the bolster cover, right sides together. Machine stitch, easing the fabric as you work. Repeat for the other end of the bolster.

7 Turn the cover through to the right side and neaten the free raw edges by machining a zigzag stitch, or turning a narrow hem to the wrong side. Run a gathering thread around each opening using strong thread (A).

8 Insert the bolster in the cover and draw up the gathering threads as tightly as possible, finishing off with several stitches to secure the centre. Distribute gathers evenly. Stitch a tassel over each end to hide the join (B).

B. Neaten the joins by attaching a tassel to each end.

fitted CHAIR COVER

Dress up your living room chairs and give them a new lease of life with a stylish cover. The basic pattern can be adapted to fit any straight-backed, armless chair.

You will need

CHAIR COVER FABRIC, SEE MEASURING, OVERLEAF

CONTRASTING BOW FABRIC

PATTERN PAPER

TAPE MEASURE

PENCIL

SCISSORS

PINS

MATCHING THREADS

SEWING MACHINE

IRON AND BOARD

Furnishing fabrics can transform the look of a room, and fabric covers in particular can be very effective in pulling together an odd assortment of living room or kitchen chairs into a single style.

Consider the decor and also the dimensions of your room when choosing a fabric. The overall design and texture of the fabric should coordinate well with the existing colour scheme. Striped fabrics can be a good choice for a small room as they emphasise the vertical line of the chair, drawing the eye upwards. Plain or textured fabrics tend to give a softened look which may increase the visual size of the room, while patterns can make a large room feel more cozy.

Choose a medium-weight furnishing fabric that washes and wears well – chair covers are likely to require laundering from time to time due to spills. Make sure that the material is heavy enough to hang well without being bulky. Cotton or chintz works very well – you could even use ticking or unbleached calico.

A striped fabric will emphasize the straight line of a chair, giving it visual height.

47

chapter three

making the chair cover

If you are planning to use an expensive fabric, you may want to make a practice cover with an old sheet before cutting out.

MEASURING AND CUTTING OUT

1 Using the diagrams below as a guide, measure each section of the chair. Add 1.5cm / ½in seam allowances to measurements of all the outer edges. Note that the 'inside back panel' piece must include the width of the seat back at side and top edges. You will need approximately 2m x 150cm / 2¼ yds x 60in wide fabric for the cover plus a strip of contrasting fabric for the bows measuring 75 x 16cm / 30 x 7in.

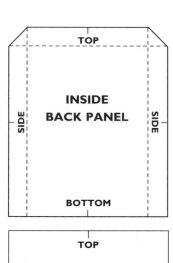

The amount of material you need for the cover will depend on the dimensions of your chair. Be careful to take accurate measurements so that the finished cover fits snugly over the chair and the overall look is professional.

2 Transfer the measurements to paper and cut out pattern for each piece. For the corner panels, cut patterns measuring 20cm / 8in wide by the front skirt height.

3 Pin paper patterns to fabric, following the straight grain and matching any pattern repeats. If fabric has large design motifs, make sure they are positioned centrally on each pattern piece. Cut out fabric pieces and mark middle points of all pieces as shown on templates.

TOP · CORNER PANEL · CORNER PANEL

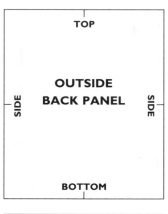

TOP
OUTSIDE BACK PANEL
SIDE · SIDE
BOTTOM

TOP
INSIDE BACK PANEL
SIDE · SIDE
BOTTOM

TOP · CORNER PANEL · CORNER PANEL

TOP
FRONT SKIRT PANEL

TOP
BACK SKIRT PANEL

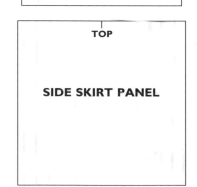

TOP
SEAT PANEL
SIDE · SIDE
BOTTOM

TOP
SIDE SKIRT PANEL

TOP
SIDE SKIRT PANEL

MAKING THE CHAIR COVER

1 Use a 1.5cm / ½in seam allowance throughout. With the right sides together, stitch the top corners of 'inside back panel' to form the top chair corners.

A. Mark the middle points of 'seat panel' and 'inside back panel' on the fabric so that they match up.

2 With right sides of fabric together and with middle points matching, stitch the top edge of 'seat panel' to the bottom edge of 'inside back panel' (A).

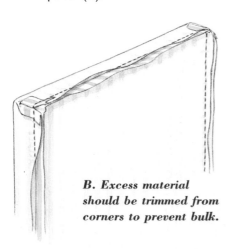

B. Excess material should be trimmed from corners to prevent bulk.

3 With right sides of the fabric together, pin 'outside back panel' to 'inside back panel' along the sides and top edge, matching middle points on both pieces. Stitch, easing around corners and trim (B), to form the back cover.

4 To neaten 'back', 'front' and 'side skirt panels', turn in, press and stitch a double hem around the side and bottom edges.

5 With right sides of fabric together, stitch top of 'front skirt' to front edge of 'seat panel', both 'side skirt' pieces to side edges of 'seat panel' and 'back skirt' to edge of 'outside back panel', matching middle points.

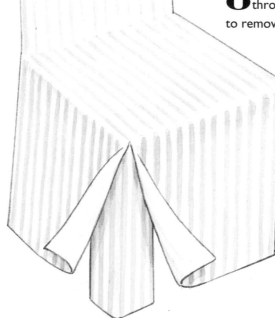

Crafty tip

If using a plain fabric, you can topstitch the chair cover hems and seam edges with heavyweight thread in a contrasting colour. Make the bows in the same colour to complement the chair covers.

6 To neaten 'corner panels', turn in, press and stitch a double hem around all four side and bottom edges. Centre each front corner panel between 'front' and 'side skirt panels', so that each corner panel lies behind a skirt opening. Stitch right side 'corner panel' to wrong side 'seat panel' (C).

7 Centre each back corner panel between back and side skirt panels, with right side of corner panel against wrong side of side panels. Stitch the top to the bottom of the inside and outside back panels.

8 Trim seams; turn the cover through to the right side. Press to remove any creases.

C. The 'corner panels' are sewn inside all seat corners to hide the legs of the chair.

9 Cut two strips of contrasting fabric for the bows, each measuring 75 x 8cm / 30 x 3½in. Fold each strip in half, so that right sides of the fabric are together. Stitch across one end and along the length of the strip. Turn through to the right side; turn in and stitch the open end closed. Fold each strip in half, then hand stitch the fold to the top of both back skirt openings (D). Tie into bows.

D. Sew centre of bow strip to corner point at 'outside back' and 'back skirt panel'.

Chair covers made with the same striped fabric in two coordinating colours can make an appealing contrast.

final touch

Instead of using the same fabric for the bows, use woven or shiny ribbon in a contrasting colour; or use thick, silky cord with tassels added to the ends.

lamp shade MAKE OVER

Use a variety of textured and decorated papers to cover a lampshade for a novelty finish.

O nce the fabric on a shade becomes shabby or the colours fade, you can replace it with decorative papers instead of throwing the shade out or having it re-covered with fabric.

A wide variety of textured and decorated papers is available. Choose off-white ones textured with fibre, bark, dried flowers and leaves, and include some with an imprinted pattern (these look almost like watermarks).

You can also make your own papers and decorate them, or you may prefer to add dried flowers and foliage to a ready-made paper. Two ways are used to attach the paper panels to the frame. They are alternated, with one paper panel glued around the metal support of the shade, followed by one trimmed to fit within the frame and secured with raffia.

The lamp stand was originally stained dark brown. It was decorated with a novelty paint finish. A deep red paint was used and the raised areas were highlighted with gilt cream. Dried red and pink rose petals were added to a paper panel on the lampshade to complement the colour of the stand.

chapter three

decorating the lampshade

The frame shown is 25cm / 10in in diameter at the top and 51cm / 20in at the bottom, and has eight upright supports 35.5 / 14in long.

1 To make the paper panels secured with glue, lay the shade on its side on a piece of plain paper and draw the outline of one section. Remove the frame and draw a line 12mm / ½in larger all round. Cut out the template and check that it fits alternate panels.

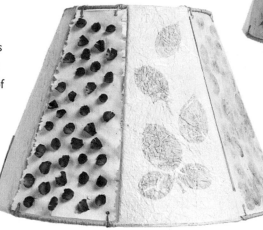

Dried rose petals on the front of a panel and dried leaves at the back.

3 Repeat at the bottom, again folding and cutting the paper to fit between the uprights. Glue the edges to the back of the paper, keeping the tension tight.

4 Make cuts along the sides parallel to the top and bottom to remove the corners and so that the paper fits neatly between the top and bottom rings. Fold the paper back behind the uprights and glue in place. Leave to dry.

5 For the remaining four panels, place the shade on the template and draw the inside outline of a panel on it. Trim it and check it fits neatly in the open panels without overlapping the frame.

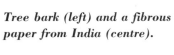

Tree bark (left) and a fibrous paper from India (centre).

2 Cut four pieces of your chosen papers. Tape them temporarily to an upright on either side with masking tape, on alternate panels. Make cuts along the sides at the top so that when you fold the paper edge over the frame it fits between the two uprights. Glue the edges in place and leave to dry.

Craftytip

You can use this method to renovate almost any shade provided you use the shade to cut accurate templates.

6 Cover the exposed parts at the top and bottom of the frame with raffia. Start by trapping the end of the raffia under itself and winding it around the frame. Glue the other end in place and leave to dry before trimming the ends.

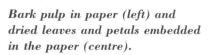

Bark pulp in paper (left) and dried leaves and petals embedded in the paper (centre).

7 Use the template to cut four panels in your chosen papers. Punch two holes 18mm / ¾in in along each top and bottom edge.

8 Take a length of raffia and tie a knot in one end. Thread the other end through a hole in the paper. Repeat with all the holes. Place the paper panels in position and secure the tops by tying the raffia to the raffia-covered frame. Repeat at the bottom to complete the frame.

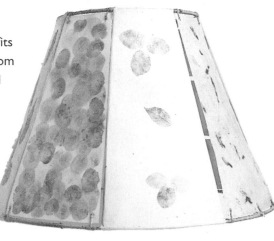

Rose petals (left) glued to the back of a paper panel.

9 If using rose petals, glue these randomly to one or two of the panels. You can use them on the outside of the paper panels or on the inside, along with leaves. The petals will show through the paper panel when the lamp is in use.

bamboo table MAKEOVER

A junk shop find is given a new lease of life with two shades of green paint used for the base coat, which is then decorated with a blossom motif.

The table has bamboo legs and edgings, but you can apply the paint finish to any small wooden table. The table, which had no previous finish, was simply wiped down and the top surface lightly sanded to key it for the paint. If necessary, use a little filler to make good any cracks or indentations, although with this finish, small imperfections won't detract from the overall appearance.

An acrylic primer and emulsion paint are used for the background, which is then decorated freehand with a sprig of blossoms. Don't be daunted when doing the freehand decoration – copy the motif (see overleaf) on to the table using tracing down paper, and then paint it in stages, doing all the green stems and leaves first before adding the pink and the finishing touches. Black acrylic paint is used for the details, but you may find it easier doing this with a fine black felt-tip pen.

You will need

- BAMBOO TABLE
- MEDIUM- AND FINE-GRADE SANDPAPER
- ACRYLIC PRIMER
- PAINTBRUSH
- CLOTH
- TWO SHADES OF GREEN MATT EMULSION PAINT
- SMALL ARTIST'S PAINTBRUSH
- CLEAR MATT ACRYLIC VARNISH
- TRACING PAPER
- PENCIL
- TRACING DOWN PAPER
- BLACK AND TWO SHADES OF PINK ARTIST'S ACRYLIC PAINT
- INDELIBLE FINE BLACK FELT-TIP PEN, OPTIONAL

53

chapter three

decorating the bamboo table

Wipe the table down and, if necessary, sand it to remove any previous finish, and to key or prime the surface. Enlarge the motif, as necessary, to fit the table top. To do this, see Enlarging a Design, p6.

1 Paint the whole table with a coat of acrylic primer. Leave the primer to dry then apply a second coat. Leave to dry.

2 Paint the table with the paler shade of green emulsion paint. When dry, apply a second coat and leave to dry.

3 Using a damp cloth, apply the darker shade of green by wiping it on in streaks over the table top and shelf. Do this along the lengths of the surfaces.

4 Use a small paintbrush to apply darker green to the bamboo rings along the legs and to the rings on the edging of the top. Leave to dry then apply two coats of varnish, leaving the first to dry before applying the second.

5 Trace or photocopy the blossom motif and check that the size is suitable for decorating the table top. Transfer it to the surface using tracing down paper. Repeat on the shelf below.

6 Using a small artist's paintbrush and the paler shade of green paint, paint the leaves and the stems of the motif. Leave to dry.

7 Paint the blossoms in pale pink. When dry, outline them in the darker pink. When dry, paint the stamens black (or use a black felt-tip pen). Leave until dry.

8 Apply two coats of varnish, leaving the first to dry before adding the second.

Copy the motif, enlarge it as necessary, to fit the table, and paint it freehand.

a classic fabric
LAMPSHADE

Make this Empire shade using a frame, old or new. Choose your own plain or patterned fabric and trim according to your decor.

The Empire lampshade is a classic, both in its curved form and as the straight-sided version shown here. Making your own shade on a wire frame gives you the opportunity to create a perfect match with the rest of your decor and use beautiful fabrics – such as the silk used here – to give a touch of real elegance.

When choosing fabrics, keep in mind the brightness of the light you require. Dark fabrics mute the lamplight considerably more than paler, translucent ones, though they can be lined with a lighter colour to reflect more light. Bedrooms usually have softer lighting, while a reading lamp needs to be brighter.

making a lampshade

Use the wire frame as a guide to creating your pattern. This needs to be exact, so measure carefully and cut the fabric accordingly to ensure a neat, smooth finish.

1 To make sewing easier and to keep the cover in place, tape the top and bottom rings of the frame tightly with binding tape. The length of tape you need is twice the circumference of the rings. Start at one of the upright struts (A) and finish by securing the end with a couple of stitches. Bind two upright struts opposite each other. Secure ends with a figure eight knot (to be undone later).

A. To start the binding, fold the tape over itself to secure the end.

STOP

Check as you bind the frame that it is completely covered with the tape.

2 Make a pattern out of the calico, cutting the fabric across the grain. To do this, place one corner over the top ring between the two taped struts so that you have sufficient width to reach the taped struts. Pin the fabric to the side struts, starting at a corner and adjusting the fabric as you go. Pin the top and bottom, pulling the calico so there are no creases.

3 Mark the corners with a pencil. Unpin the calico. Join up the four marked corners with straight lines to outline the pattern. Cut out along marked lines. Fold the shade fabric in half, right sides facing, and place the calico pattern on it across the grain. Pin the double thickness of fabric together around, not on, the pattern (B). Mark the corners with a pencil. Cut out the fabric, leaving a 5cm / 2in border all round the pattern.

4 Sew the side edges together, matching the pencil corner marks, with small zig-zag stitches. Trim the seams down to 6mm / ¼ in. Remove binding tape from the upright struts. Place fabric over the frame, side seams to the struts. Pin corner marks on fabric to the binding on the rings. Pin fabric to binding on top and bottom rings, pulling the material to give a smooth finish. Stitch right to left around both rings, removing pins as you go. Cut away excess fabric, holding scissors against the frame.

B. Pin the fabric around the pattern and mark the corners.

5 Make the lining in the same way. Insert lining into frame between gimbal (the ring that fits over the bulb) and struts. Match seam to seam and pin. Make a small cut in the lining where the gimbal joins the frame. Pull the lining taut over the rings, adjusting the pins to get a good fit. Stitch as before.

6 Make a small bias from the lining fabric: cut 7.5 x 2.5cm / 3 x 1in fabric across the grain, folding the sides in lengthways to hide the raw edges. Press with your fingers and position under the fitting to cover the slits in the lining (C). Stitch the two ends to the top ring. Attach braid to both rings with fabric glue to hide stitching.

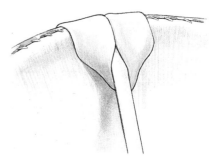

C. Fold the bias around the gimbal to conceal the slit in the lining.

jugs of FLOWERS

Jugs come in all sizes and shapes and lend themselves to pretty informal fresh flower displays.

Jug arrangements shouldn't be too formal – the lines should be loose and quite flowing. When making jug arrangements, look at the size and colour of the jug first. The colour is important – if it is heavily patterned, keep the arrangement of colours simple – white flowers and plenty of green foliage work well.

Where the jug has a simple pattern, you can pick out the colours in the flowers – use a bunch of yellow tulips, for example, to form the centre-piece of a medium-sized jug arrangement (see overleaf), picking up the colours from the jug pattern. Unusual small irises, black and green in colour, are used to add tiny points of contrast. The blue-green of the eucalyptus foliage adds another colour dimension.

Small jugs demand simple arrangements. Look for flowers to provide an upright spiky look, in this case, black irises (see overleaf). Fluid lines are created with foliage, such as tree ivy, with black berries that echo the colour of the irises. Be generous with the foliage to create a soft outline.

arranging flowers in jugs

Filling large jugs can be expensive. Look to your garden for supplies, especially for foliage, and use flowers with a simple colour theme, according to what is in season.

LARGE JUG

Gypsophila, fresh wheat, Veronica (white spikes) and white roses are used in this display (below).

The Veronica serves two purposes. The foliage is quite dense and helps to fill the arrangement, while the spikes help to draw the eye, as does the wheat. The roses add small solid focal points of colour and the delicate gypsophila softens the overall effect.

JUG WITH NUGGETS

Black irises and tree ivy with berries are used here (above).

As the jug is small, the flowers and foliage are limited. Glass nuggets anchor the stems. The berries on the ivy complement the irises, keeping the display uncluttered and simple.

PATTERNED JUG

Yellow tulips, black irises and eucalyptus are used here (above). The yellow tulips complement the yellow on the jug and contrast with the blue. The black irises add shape and the eucalyptus foliage fills out and softens the display.

USING JUGS

As jugs have wide mouths, arrangements tend to fall away from the centre. There are two ways of dealing with this. You should start with the foliage to create a base (the stems will help to anchor the flowers in the jug) and finish with it, if necessary, to fill out any gaps in the display. If the arrangement has a tendency to fall to one side, as in the case of a small jug, and you don't want to overwhelm it with greenery, you can use glass nuggets or scrunched up chicken wire to support the stems. In the case of clear glass jugs, use glass nuggets in simple colours, such as blue and green, or clear glass, and avoid colours such as red that may distract the eye from the actual display.

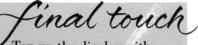

final touch
Top up the display with water frequently and keep it out of direct sunlight or draughts to prolong the life of the flowers.

simple ragging

Of all decorative paint finishes, ragging is one of the simplest. The technique shown here, ideal for giving new life to furniture, uses water-based glaze and provides a perfect background to stencilling.

You can transform almost any small household items, as well as walls, by ragging them. You just brush a coat of glaze on to a base coat, then lift the still-wet paint off using a lint-free rag to produce a mottled finish. The final effect is more or less bold depending on what you use to lift off the glaze – this can be a rag, a plastic bag or some crumpled paper.

The glaze can be coloured either with a matt emulsion paint or a small amount of colourizer, depending on the brand used. Water-based glaze, also known as scumble, and colourizer are available from specialist paint shops. The glaze can be wiped clean but is not sufficiently hard wearing to be scrubbed. Apply a coat of water-based varnish to seal the surface.

COLOUR EFFECTS

The glaze is usually tinted a slightly darker shade than the base coat. For a more striking effect, try using a different coloured glaze or, once the first coat of glaze has been applied and ragged off, leave it to dry thoroughly then apply a second glaze in a different colour and rag it off.

RAGGING IS SUITABLE FOR • a wide range of surfaces, such as furniture • lamp bases • trays • storage containers • any firm surface, including walls, that is suitable for emulsion paint.

$\mathbf{Y}$ou can rag on an existing paint surface if you're happy with the colour. Otherwise repaint it with vinyl silk emulsion and leave it to dry overnight. Tint the glaze a slightly darker shade than the base coat. Repeat the ragging in another colour for added interest.

ALTERNATIVE EFFECTS

For a bolder effect, use a plastic bag crumpled into a rough ball. You need a plentiful supply as plastic does not absorb paint as rags do.

1 To colour the glaze, mix a small amount of matt emulsion or colourizer into the emulsion or glaze. Stir well so that the colour is evenly blended. Apply the glaze with sweeping, criss-cross brush strokes, working on one self-contained area at a time.

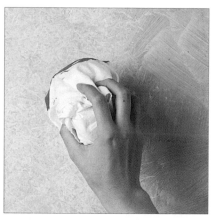

2 Take a clean rag and crumple it. Then dab randomly at the painted surface to lift off some of the wet glaze.

For a fine textured look, use a twill or cord fabric.

▽ STOP

Before you start ragging, make sure you have enough clean, lint-free rags at hand to enable you to complete the whole project.

*Crafty*tip

If some areas look too thin or uneven, apply another layer of glaze and rag again, while the glaze is still wet.

3 Keep turning and re-folding the rag. When soaked, discard it and start with a new rag. Carry on until the whole surface has been ragged.

4 If excess glaze builds up in corners and along edges, blend it in using a small stippling brush or a long-bristled household paintbrush.

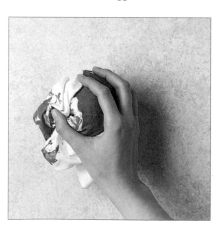

THE DINING ROOM

The Dining Room

CONTENTS

unlined curtains

Some rooms, especially those with small windows, benefit from unlined curtains which allow some light to filter through. Choose patterned or plain lightweight fabrics.

Fabrics such as voile, lace or medium-weight cottons are ideal for unlined curtains. Allow one and a half to two times the length of the track to calculate the number of fabric widths required.

The drop is determined by the heading and whether the curtains are to be hung from a pole, rod or ceiling track system. With standard heading tape, the drop is from the top of the rod or track. With pencil or pleated heading tape, the drop is 2.5cm / 1in above the rod or track. With a pole, the drop is taken to the floor plus 10-15cm / 4-6in. In a recess, allow 6mm / ¼in from the sill. Add on 25-30cm / 10-12in for the hems.

With patterned fabric, you need to match the pattern. As a guide, for every fabric width, buy one extra repeat, minus one. So, for a pair of curtains four widths wide, buy three extra repeats. If necessary, match patterns vertically and horizontally. Checks must match vertically and horizontally so that the pattern matches at the centre where the curtains meet. To join curtains, use flat fell seams or French seams. Use standard or pencil-pleat heading tape at the top. **USE UNLINED CURTAINS** • where you want an airy effect • on small windows • where privacy isn't a problem.

You will need

TAPE MEASURE, PINS AND SCISSORS

FABRIC AND MATCHING THREAD

SEWING MACHINE

HEADING TAPE

IRON

*A*s for the curtains, allow 1½ - 2 times the length of the curtain track for the heading tape. Check when buying that this is sufficient as some types of heading tape require more, depending on the type of pleat. If you need to use half widths of fabric, add these to the outside edges. Cut the fabric straight and mark the hem line. Cut across 15cm / 6in below this. To match a pattern, lay this length alongside the remaining fabric and cut another length, lining up the design. Cut the required number of lengths in the same way.

1 Fold and press up to 2.5cm / 1in seam allowance to the wrong side of the fabric. Place it over another length, matching the pattern (vertical patterns may require enlarging the seam allowances). Align and pin along noticeable pattern details.

FLAT FELL SEAMS

Place the right sides of the fabric together, edges even, and stitch along the seam line. Trim one edge of the fabric to within 3mm / ⅛in of the sewing line. Press raw edges to one side so that the wider edge lies on top. Turn this edge under the narrower edge and machine stitch close to the folded edge. Press with an iron.

FRENCH SEAMS

Place the wrong sides of the fabric together with the edges even. Stitch along the seam line then trim to within 3mm / ⅛in of the sewing line. Press the seam open and turn the right sides together, enclosing the raw edges. Machine stitch along the seam line.

2 Fold the top length back, right sides together, and pin along the selvedges (side edges), setting the pins horizontally. Pin the fabric at regular intervals.

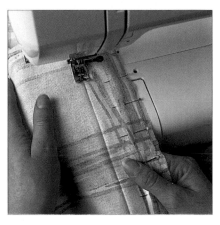

3 If using patterned fabric, remove the pins that were keeping the pattern matched, and machine stitch along the crease line, using a small stitch.

Craftytip

On small curtains or windows in obscure positions, you can cheat by pinking the raw edges of the seams, or even simply oversewing the seams to neaten them.

Triple pleats: curtain width required is twi the length of the curtain track.

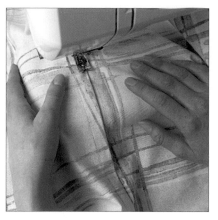

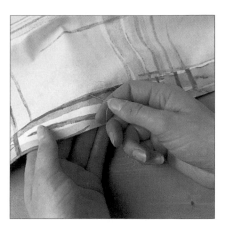

4 To join the fabric with a flat fell seam, trim one raw edge to 2cm / ³⁄₄in. The other raw edge needs to be narrower. Trim it down to 3mm / ¹⁄₈in.

5 Fold and press the wide edge over the narrower one so that the top edge encloses the narrow edge. Stitch close to the fold and press.

6 For the side hem, press 6mm / ¹⁄₄in to the wrong side. Press under another 12mm / ¹⁄₂in. Pin to match pattern. Tack in place and machine stitch.

7 Fold a 5cm / 2in single hem allowance to the wrong side at the top of the curtain. Mitre the corner neatly to remove the excess fabric. Pin the fabric in place. Cut the heading tape to the width of the curtain, plus 5cm / 2in.

8 With the heading tape across the top width of the curtain, turn under 2.5cm / 1in at each end of the tape and ease the cords free at the ends. Pin the heading tape in place, covering the raw edges.

9 Machine stitch the heading tape in place, sewing close to the top edge. Repeat with the other edge, working in the same direction. Knot the loose cords at the edge which will be the centre of the curtains.

HEADING TAPES

Pencil pleats: requires curtain width of 2¼–2½ times the length of curtain track.

Cartridge pleats: requires curtain width twice the length of the curtain track.

10 Pull up the cords from the other end of the heading tape until the curtain is the width required. Space the gathers evenly and secure the loose ends of the cord, tying firmly.

11 Insert curtain hooks into the pockets on the heading tape at regular intervals. Don't space the hooks too far apart or the curtains will not hang well.

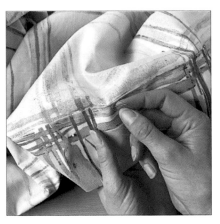

Craftytip

Tack the bottom hem and hang the curtains for one or two days to allow the fabric to drop. Then adjust the length and sew the hem by hand.

12 Turn under about 15cm / 6in at the bottom of the curtains to form a double hem. Pin and tack, then hang the curtains for a few days to allow them to drop.

final touch

If you want to use tiebacks with unlined curtains, don't use anything too formal or too large. Any leftover fabric can be used to make tiebacks, or use ribbon.

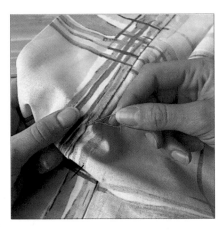

13 Take the curtains down again to complete the hem. Hand sew the bottom edge using hem stitch and remove the tacking. Press with a warm iron.

porphyry
LAMPBASE

This classic shape for a lampbase is given a rich and handsome finish with porphyry, making it an eye-catching feature on an occasional table.

It is well worth taking the time to decorate a lampbase with the porphyry technique. Use an old base that's seen better days or buy a cheap one and give it an expensive looking finish. Work around the base, adding a layer of colour at a time. Remember that the closer you are, the bigger the marks will be.

You will need to work quickly and efficiently so that as much as possible of the paint is still wet by the time you get to the stage of spattering the white spirit. This will break up the surface of the paint layers and give a very natural stone effect.

You will need

TABLE LAMPBASE

FINE SANDPAPER

MASKING TAPE

OIL-BASED WHITE UNDERCOAT

2.5CM / 1IN PAINTBRUSH

WIRE WOOL

SCUMBLE GLAZE

OIL PAINTS IN ALIZARIN CRIMSON, YELLOW OCHRE, RAW UMBER AND WHITE

OLD BRUSH

WHITE SPIRIT

NO 9 FITCH BRUSH

GOLD POWDER OR GOLD OIL-BASED PAINT

TOOTHBRUSH

SATIN OR GLOSS VARNISH

painting the lampbase

If possible, remove the fittings and flex from the base. Place it on a thick telephone directory so it can be turned easily and cover the work area with old newspapers.

1 Make sure that the surface of the lamp is dry, clean and smooth. Use fine sandpaper to sand it down, if necessary. Tape up the flex, element and the bottom of the lamp with masking tape (A). Paint a coat of white/off-white oil-based paint, using the 2.5cm / 1in brush. When dry, sand down with very fine sandpaper or wire wool.

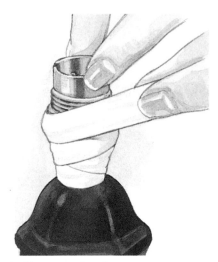

A. Tape up the element.

2 For the base coat, mix four parts scumble glaze with three parts alizarin crimson, paint over the under-coat and leave to dry. Mix up the first spatter coat (three parts white spirit to one part raw umber and a touch of white) and spatter evenly by knocking the brush gently against another brush.

3 It is not necessary to wait for the paint to dry between the

Whoops

Have a cotton cloth handy in case the spatters are too big – just mop them up and re-spatter.

layers of spattering. Mix another runny mixture of ochre and a touch of white oil paint and white spirit. Use a fitch brush to spatter a fine speckle over the lamp by gently pulling back the hairs of the brush. Very sparingly, spatter a layer of gold, this time using a toothbrush (B).

B. Pull back the bristles of a toothbrush to spatter on a fine spray of gold paint.

The porphyry effect is built up with layers of spattered colour to produce a rich, dark red flecked with subtle speckles of gold.

Crafty tip

Dilute the paint if necessary – the thinner it is, the finer the spatter will be.

4 Mix a runny mixture of pink, using crimson, a touch of white and a little yellow ochre and white spirit, and spatter.

5 While the paint is still wet, spatter with white spirit, using a fitch brush. Leave to dry. Paint the whole base with satin or gloss varnish. When dry, repeat with another layer.

dining chair MAKEOVER

Whether it's worn or you simply fancy a change of colour, the drop-in seat of a dining chair is easy to re-cover. And while you're at it, spruce up the woodwork, too.

Before you do anything to a chair, check that it is not an antique. The standard dining chair has a drop-in seat that is easily removed by pushing it out from the bottom. The seat frame may have webbing to support a stuffing, which is covered with calico with the seat cover on top of this. All of this depends on any previous restoration.

Remove the seat and strip it down. Take notes as you do this with diagrams of any details, such as how the corners are folded, and the order in which the seat is built up. If the frame has webbing, check whether this has to be replaced or not. Instead of webbing, the seat may have a solid base or a frame covered with plywood (these are the easiest to re-cover). If you want to reuse the original stuffing, allow for a calico lining. Otherwise, replace it with wadding – use a heavy weight and double it up if necessary. The original tacks will probably have to be renewed – buy the same length or use heavy-duty staples instead.

You will need

CHAIR WITH DROP-IN SEAT

PAINT OR VARNISH STRIPPER

SANDPAPER

WOOD STAIN AND VARNISH

TACK LIFTER OR PLIERS

SMALL HAMMER AND TACKS OR HEAVY-DUTY STAPLER

250G / 10OZ WADDING

3MM PLYWOOD OR WOVEN WEBBING, TO COVER SEAT FRAME

HESSIAN, IF USING WEBBING

CALICO, IF USING ORIGINAL STUFFING

UPHOLSTERY FABRIC

STRONG THREAD AND LARGE-EYED NEEDLE

UPHOLSTERY BUTTONS (OPTIONAL)

MATCHSTICK

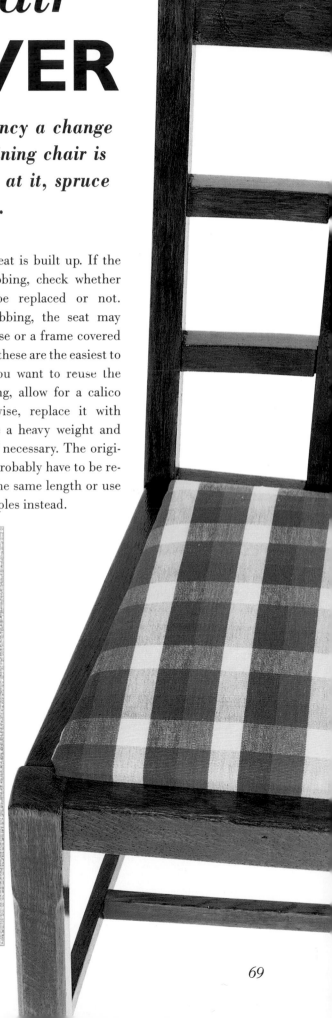

doing the makeover

Remove the seat and make good the chair frame. Do this first so that any varnish or paint is completely dry when the seat is re-covered.

1 Strip the seat frame and smooth any rough edges with sandpaper. Compare the new cover fabric against the old. If the fabrics are of a similar weight, the seat should fit, otherwise you may have to plane or sand the seat frame first. Test by folding the fabric over the frame and checking that it fits in the chair frame.

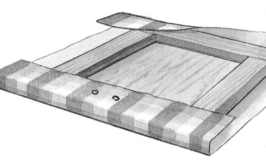

A. Start tacking the fabric from the centre outwards.

2 If using webbing, tack it in place, following the same pattern as the original and keeping the tension even. Cover the webbing with hessian cut to fit the frame and tack it in place. Cut wadding to size.

3 If your chair seat has a plywood covering over the frame, cut the wadding to the same size as the seat frame.

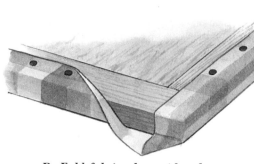

B. Fold fabric along side edge.

4 Lay the cover fabric wrong side up and place the wadding on top. Place the seat frame upside down on the wadding, keeping it centred. Pull the fabric up around the frame and make sure you have enough to fold and tack to the bottom of the frame. A 75mm / 3in allowance all round should be enough. Cut the fabric to size and reassemble the frame as before. Fold the front edge up and make a temporary tack in the centre. Repeat with the back and then the two sides. Check that any pattern or stripes are straight. Smooth the fabric over the seat, adjust the wadding and secure tacks as necessary to get an even finish.

5 Tack the fabric, starting at the centre back and working outwards (A). Leave 5cm / 2in untacked at the corner. Repeat at the front and then tack or staple the two sides, leaving 5cm / 2in untacked at the corners.

6 To finish the corners, fold the fabric to make neat mitres on the sides (B). Tack in place (C).

7 Decide where you want the buttons on the top and measure and mark these points on the bottom. With a plywood base, drill 3mm / ⅛in holes, using a collar

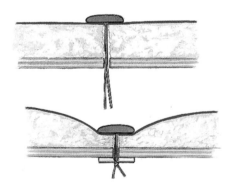

C. Tack the folded fabric corners.

around the bit so as not to drill into the cover fabric. Pull a needle threaded with strong thread through from the bottom to the top. Thread the button and then take the needle to the bottom. Wrap thread around half a matchstick to tighten it (D). Repeat with remaining buttons.

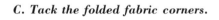

D. Tighten the thread with the matchstick to indent the wadding.

You will need

Two 40x40cm / 15³⁄₄x15³⁄₄in pieces of white 22 count Hardanger fabric

Tacking cotton in a contrasting colour

Matching sewing thread, needle and pins

Square embroidery frame or embroidery hoop

1 skein white DMC pearl cotton

Size 22 tapestry needle

Sharp pair of scissors with fine points

Sewing machine

Iron

30x30cm / 12x12in cushion pad

hardanger CUSHION COVER

Hardanger embroidery is a type of cutwork traditionally worked by the people of Hardanger, on the west coast of Norway.

Worked in the traditional white-on-white combination of thread and fabric, this Hardanger design uses 36 groups of four Kloster blocks which are placed edge-to-edge in a square. The centre of 16 of the Kloster blocks are cut away to make a lacy design and the square is bordered with satin stitch triangles. The cushion cover has been worked on special Hardanger fabric, but you can use an evenweave linen of a similar count instead.

71

making the cushion cover

The cover is made from an evenweave linen, with one or both sides embroidered. A cushion pad is inserted to complete the project.

1 Fold one piece of the Hardanger fabric into quarters to find the centre and mark it with a few stitches. Mount the fabric in the frame or hoop. Work groups of four Kloster blocks as shown on the chart below, working each seven-stitch block over six vertical and six horizontal threads. Start at the centre and work outwards, taking care to count the threads accurately, noting that the chart shows one quarter of the complete design.

2 Remove the fabric from the frame and cut away the areas marked in red on the chart. Put the fabric back in the frame and work the triangular satin stitch blocks round the edge of the embroidery and the small square block in each of the corners.

3 Trim away the surplus fabric round both pieces of fabric to leave two pieces of fabric each 35cm / 13¾in square. Place the two pieces together with right sides facing and pin round the edge.

4 Using matching sewing thread, machine stitch twice round the edge of the fabric taking a seam allowance of 1.5cm / ⅝in and leaving a 20cm / 8in gap in the stitching at the centre of one side.

5 Trim away the fabric slightly at each corner to avoid bulk, turn the cover to the right side, and press. Insert the cushion pad through the opening and slip stitch the opening closed.

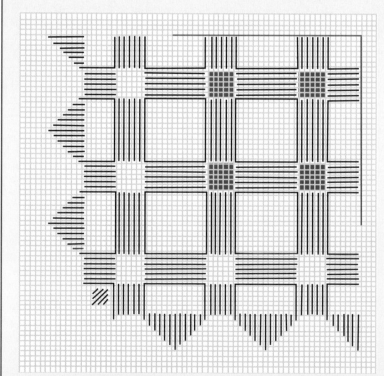

Chart to work the cover

circular
TABLECLOTH

*Fancy making your own tablecloth? Just choose
the colour and fabric to suit your room, make
a few basic calculations and start stitching!*

First decide on the length of tablecloth. For a small occasional table the cloth often looks best if it just clears the floor. For a dining table, a shorter drop is best.

For the length of fabric, measure the diameter of the table top. Decide on the overhang excluding the frill. Add 1.5cm / ½in hem allowance. Double this number and add it to the diameter of the table top. Double this total to give you the length of fabric required excluding the frill. For the frill, decide on the depth (15cm / 6in is usual). Add 3cm / 1¼in for the hem. For the full length, make up the pattern (see Step 1 overleaf) and measure the curve. Multiply it by six and work out how many strips for the frill you can cut from the fabric width. Multiply the number of strips by the width of the frill and add this to the fabric for the overall total.

making the tablecloth

For the pattern: use a square of paper slightly larger than half the cloth diameter without the frill. Tie one end of a piece of string around a pencil and pin the other end into the corner of the paper. The distance between the pin and pencil should be half the cloth diameter, plus a hem allowance of 1.5cm / ½in, minus the frill depth.

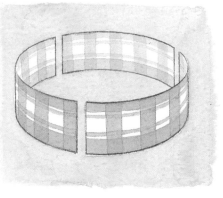

1 Hold the drawing pin in place. Draw an arc with the pencil from one side of the paper to the other (A). Remove the pin and string and cut along the arc. This gives you a pattern equal to one quarter of the cloth, minus the frill.

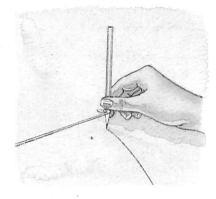

A. Draw an arc from one side of the paper to the other.

2 Fold the fabric in half lengthways and widthways. Place pattern on fabric, matching corners to folded corner of cloth. Pin and cut out, along the curve. Remove pattern and unfold fabric.

B. Tack and stitch the hem in place after pinning.

3 Stitch all round the tablecloth 1.5cm / ½in from outer edge. Turn back hem along stitched line, then tuck under raw edge to half the hem width. Pin, tack and stitch the hem in place for a neat, self finish (B).

4 For the frill, cut the strips according to the width required plus a hem allowance. You need one and a half times the length of the circumference of the cloth. Pin, tack and stitch the frill lengths together to form a ring (C).

Craftytip

Use leftover fabric to make matching napkins, cushions or lampshades.

C. Pin, tack and stitch frill lengths together so that they form a ring.

5 Turn under a double 6mm / ¼in hem along both edges of the frill. Pin, tack and stitch hems in place. Fold the frill into four equal sections and mark with pins.

6 Work two rows of gathering stitches along each section of the frill. Position first row 2.5cm / 1in from top hem and second row 3cm / 1¼in from top hem (D). Pull up gathers in each section to quarter circumference of tablecloth.

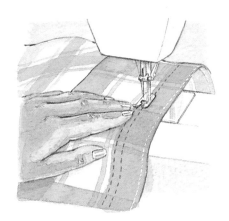

D. Work two rows of gathering stitches along each section of frill.

7 Place the wrong side of the frill to the right side of the tablecloth, overlapping the top edge 1.5cm / ½in. Spacing gathers evenly, pin, tack and topstitch the frill between the gathering stitches.

white lilies

There is something very refreshing and restful about a display of all white flowers. Create a vase of formal lilies with a little support from some adhesive tape to hold them in position.

Lilies have a very dramatic appearance with their big blousy flowers and angular leaves. They are the perfect partners to foliage, as the green and white colours complement each other beautifully. Using one type and colour of flower gives the arrangement great elegance. To show it at its best, place the arrangement on a sideboard or table where it can be viewed from the side rather than from above. **USE THIS ARRANGEMENT** • on a table on its own • as a formal decoration.

You will need

TWO OR THREE LILY STEMS

FOLIAGE STEM

CARPET MOSS

IVY TRAILS

TALL GLASS VASE

DRY CLOTH

CLEAR ADHESIVE TAPE

FLORIST'S SCISSORS

Condition both flowers and foliage before arranging them by trimming the stalk ends and soaking for a couple of hours. Creating an adhesive tape framework allows you to position the flowers in the way you want to, and not the way that the shape of the vase dictates. This method works very well for glass containers as the stems are visible and they can be arranged in an attractive way.

Craftytip

Remove the stamens from the lilies prior to arrangement as they have a yellow pollen that stains if it comes in contact with clothing.

1 Fill a tall clear glass vase with water to about 50mm / 2in below the level of the brim. Dry the outside of the vase. Then, using clear adhesive tape, form a lattice across the width and length of the vase. Cut the adhesive tape so that about 2.5cm / 1in sticks to the vase.

2 Place the lily stems in the middle of the vase through the adhesive tape lattice. Turn them around so that the flowers and leaves face the direction that looks balanced and is the most pleasing.

3 Next poke the ivy trails and the foliage stems through the tape lattice around the lilies and arrange them so that they hang and bend gracefully.

4 To finish off, disguise any areas of the adhesive tape frame that are visible through the foliage by placing moss on top of the tape.

The oriental simplicity of the arrangement creates a very dramatic outline against a plain background.

stencilled
TRAY

You will need

BLANK CARDBOARD TRAY

WATER-BASED PAINTS IN BLUE,
GREEN AND PURPLE

STIFF PAINTBRUSH

STENCIL

STENCIL BRUSH

GLUE PEN

LUSTRE POWDER

SOFT PAINTBRUSH

POINTED ARTIST'S BRUSH

SPRAY-ON VARNISH, OPTIONAL

Washes of colour are used to create the background, which is then stencilled with fish motifs.

An underwater scene is created on a blank tray made of brown paper-coated cardboard, which provides an absorbent surface that can be sealed, or you can take advantage of the surface by layering on washes of blue and green to create the effect of a swirly watery world.

Stencil the larger fishes on to the centre of the tray, using stronger washes of colour, then add a border of smaller fishes stencilled around the raised edges of the tray. Waves, bubbles and eyes are painted in pale blue, then drawn over with a glue pen. Lustre powder is brushed over the whole tray, so that it adheres to the glue and adds a gentle sparkle to the finished piece. In this form, the tray is best used as a display item, but if you want to use it on an everyday basis, apply a couple of coats of spray-on varnish.

stencilling the tray

You can create this finish on surfaces other than the blank cardboard tray used here. If it is a wooden surface, prepare it by sanding and wiping it down before decorating.

1 Thin the water-based paints down with a little water to make washes in shades of blue, green and purple. Make the washes quite thin.

2 Using a blue wash, apply the paint in curving sweeps from side to side across the tray with a stiff brush. When dry, add sweeps of purple and leave to dry before finishing with sweeps of green (A).

A. Apply the colour washes in sweeps to resemble water.

3 Keep on building up the washes in layers, making sure they are diluted enough to allow the colours previously applied to show through. Carry on until you are happy with the finish.

4 Using diluted paint in shades of green (but not as diluted as for the washes), stencil one of the larger fishes centrally, then stencil two of the other cutouts behind this, to the top and bottom of the tray. Wash and dry the stencil, and flip it to stencil reverse images on the right-hand side of the tray.

5 Using the same green, stencil the larger fishes around the border first, leaving gaps for the smaller ones. Stencil these in when the larger fishes are dry.

6 Mix up some pale blue paint and use a small pointed brush to paint in bubbles, in rows of three for the larger fishes and two for the smaller border fishes.

7 Use the pale blue paint to add bubbles in groups around the large fish on the main surface of the tray, and to paint in random waves. Paint in the eyes of the large fish, and some tail details.

8 Use a glue pen to draw over the eyes, bubbles and waves (B). This dries clear, but while it is still tacky, use a dry soft brush to brush lustre powder all over the tray. Brush off the excess to leave the glue covered with the lustre powder. Leave to dry completely.

final touch

If you want to use the tray rather than leave it as a display item, apply a couple of light coats of spray-on varnish.

B. Draw over the eyes, bubbles and waves with a glue pen.

There is a knack to creating this decorative finish so practise it on a piece of board before attempting the real thing.

basic marbling

You will need

OIL SCUMBLE GLAZE

WHITE SPIRIT

METAL BOWL

CREAM OIL-BASED PAINT

ARTIST'S OIL COLOURS IN PAYNE'S GREY, NAPLES YELLOW, VENETIAN MARBLE AND WHITE

ACRYLIC PRIMER

PAINTBRUSH

SANDPAPER

BOILED LINSEED OIL

SOFT CLOTH

NOS. 8 AND 3 ARTIST'S BRUSHES

NATURAL SPONGE

OLD TOOTHBRUSH

Over many centuries, craftsmen and artists have perfected the art of painting false, or *faux*, marble, often so skilfully that the onlooker is deceived into thinking it is real marble. To do this requires a great deal of practice and skill. Nevertheless it is still possible to achieve an approximation using a selection of oil paints and cloths.

Successful marbling depends as much on colour and design as technique. It is common initially to make the colours far too intense and apply them too heavily. This is why it is a good idea to experiment on a piece of primed hardboard first. Marbles vary a great deal, both in colour and in form, so there is no reason why you can't make up your own. But be sure to follow the basic rules to make it look realistic.

USE MARBLING ON • doors • floors • fire surrounds • tabletops.

Oil scumble glaze, an essential element in a marbled surface, dries to a state where it becomes unworkable fairly quickly. However, it remains soluble in white spirit for quite a long time. It is then mixed with the oil paint and applied to the surface to be marbled. Veining is one of the most difficult aspects of marbling. Avoid heavy brush strokes and applying too much paint. The veins should not be equidistant or the same size, which would give it an unnatural effect.

MAKING THE OIL GLAZE

1 Mix one part oil scumble glaze and one part white spirit together in a metal bowl. Stir the mixture well until the white spirit and scumble glaze are thoroughly amalgamated.

2 Add a squeeze of oil colour and stir well. The glaze should end up with a creamy consistency. Make up a glaze of each of the three colours, adding white if you prefer a paler shade.

1 Apply two coats of acrylic primer, sanding down after each coat. Apply a coat of cream-coloured, oil-based paint. Leave to dry and sand down. Apply another coat and leave to dry.

2 To start the marbling, pour a little boiled linseed oil on to a soft cloth and use it to wipe down the surface being marbled. See Safety First, below, on how to dispose of the cloth.

3 Mix a yellow glaze. Using another soft cloth dipped in the yellow glaze, wipe rough diagonal lines across the surface. Leave for two minutes, then smudge and dab the marks to blur the lines.

WORK BOX

BRUSHES AND SPONGES

Soft-haired artist's brushes are available from art suppliers and craft shops. Natural sponges can be bought at specialist brush suppliers and, more expensively, from chemists. Be careful when applying white spirit – it should be in the form of a fine spray and not be allowed to drip from the toothbrush.

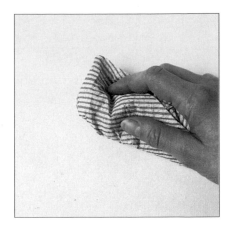

4 Using a No. 8 brush and a grey glaze, paint crooked lines, some overlapping, across the surface. Work diagonally and turn the brush as you paint, merging the lines into each other.

SAFETY FIRST

Do take care when disposing of rags soaked in boiled linseed oil as they are highly flammable. Wet the rag and place it in an empty tin or can and dispose of it outside in the rubbish bin. Don't leave it lying out in the sun.

5 Leave for 2 minutes, then take a dry brush or sponge and blur the lines, making them recede in the background. Make more blurred marks between the lines with the yellow glaze.

6 With a No. 3 brush and a red glaze, paint similar lines to those in Step 4, going in the same direction. Make them trail off to a fine point and overlap some of the grey lines.

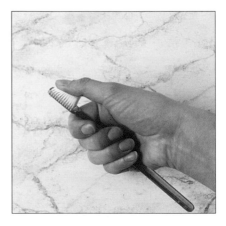

7 Leave for two minutes, and again stipple and dab the red lines using a dry sponge or soft cloth, to make them blend into the background. Use very delicate touches for a subtle effect.

8 Add more colour by dabbing a little glaze in any of the colours. When you are happy with the colour balance, use a soft cloth to smear the colours lightly, leaving a faint blur.

9 Dip the toothbrush in white spirit and spatter it over the marbling. The white spirit will spread through the mottled areas and enhance the finished marble effect.

Imitation marbling can be created in different colours and used on a variety of surfaces.

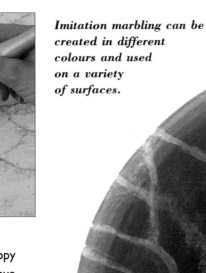

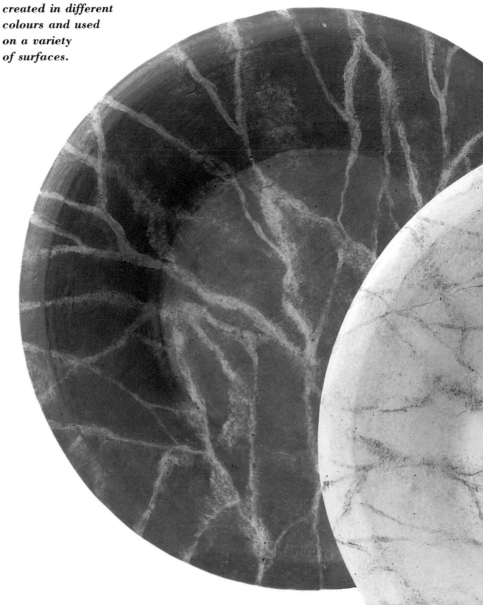

10 When you are happy with the result, leave the marbling to dry thoroughly for one or two days. Varnish with two coats of matt or satin finish varnish.

Craftytip

Once you have perfected the craft of marbling, resist overkill – too much of this effect can ruin the look and feel of a room.

chapter five

THE
KITCHEN

The Kitchen

CONTENTS

simple stencilling

Effective and decorative, stencilling is one of the best ways to give your home a personal touch.

It's easy to add both colour and style to your kitchen with the help of a stencil, a cutout of acetate or some other material. All you have to do is paint through the cut-out areas of the stencil and you can create colourful motifs and borders.

Simple and quick to use, ready-made stencils come in a wide variety of styles and patterns and help make a finished, individual look. You can apply them to almost any surface. Many come pre-cut – you just measure up and paint. Do not worry about the odd mistake as small irregularities are part of their charm.

USE STENCILS ON • tiles • kitchen cupboards • objects such as trays • fabrics • as borders on a wall • as a panel on a door.

85

U se this simple technique on flat objects such as trays and always paint on a clean, dust-free surface. *Measure up carefully – correct positioning will save time and mistakes. When you have finished wash all the brushes thoroughly, using water for water-based paints and white spirit for oil-based paints. Tie an elastic band around the bristles to keep them in place.*

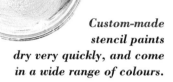

Custom-made stencil paints dry very quickly, and come in a wide range of colours.

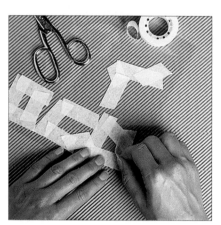

1 If your stencil is not pre-cut, fix it with masking tape to a cutting board. Lay a piece of plain paper underneath an acetate stencil so that you can see the outline of the design. Using a craft knife, cut out the areas to be painted. Always cut towards you and, when cutting curves, turn the stencil rather than the knife.

2 To avoid putting colour into the wrong stencil hole, use pieces of masking tape to cover any cut-out areas that you do not want to paint in that colour. When you get to the next colour, uncover the holes through which you want to paint and mask those you do not want to use.

Whoops

If you make a mistake when cutting your stencil, join up the cut with clear adhesive tape on both sides, then re-cut the design.

3 Measure the length of the object to be stencilled and lightly mark its midpoint with a pencil. Working from this point to the corners, calculate how many times you can fit the design on the surface, marking each stencil length. Next, mark the midpoint of the stencil sheet with a felt-tip pen. This helps line up stencil and reference marks.

WORK BOX

STENCIL BRUSHES AND PAINTS

Special stencil brushes give the best results and are the easiest to use. They are stiff and cut straight across the bristles. Buy a brush for each colour you use, in a size suitable for your design.

Stencil paints dry almost instantly, allowing you to reposition your stencil without a long wait. They are suitable for most surfaces, including walls and woodwork. To stencil on fabrics use specifically formulated fabric paints.

Craftytip

As an alternative to masking tape, use a spray adhesive that allows you to reposition the stencil. Carefully follow the manufacturers' instructions.

4 Practise your stencilling technique on a scrap of paper before you tackle your object or surface. Dip the end of the stencil brush at a right angle into the paint. Holding the brush like a pencil, work off excess paint on to a paper towel until the brush is almost dry.

▽ STOP

Before using a piece of masking tape on a painted surface, stick it on the back of your hand and tear it off a few times. This makes the tape less likely to damage the surface paint.

5 Line up the midpoint mark on the stencil with that on the object or surface you are painting. Tape the stencil down. Working with a light anti-clockwise, then clockwise motion, gradually apply the paint. Always paint from the outside edge inwards and use only small amounts of paint.

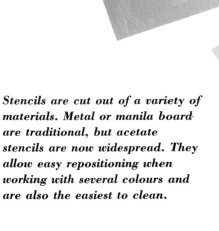

Stencils are cut out of a variety of materials. Metal or manila board are traditional, but acetate stencils are now widespread. They allow easy repositioning when working with several colours and are also the easiest to clean.

6 Rather than overload the brush, keep building up thin layers of paint in the areas where you want a deeper shade. Check your work at regular intervals by peeling back a corner of the masking tape and carefully lifting the stencil.

7 When the paint has dried, carefully peel off the masking tape and move the stencil to the next position. Tape the stencil down, following your pencil reference marks and repeat the painting process.

8 When you reach a corner, carefully position the stencil corner piece and tape into place. If your stencil does not incorporate a corner motif, pick out part of the design to use instead and arrange it to blend in with the rest of your design.

STOP
Take care not to slide the stencil when positioning or moving it across as you may smudge the paint.

Subtle painting in thin layers produces a softer, more delicate effect than heavily applied colour.

final touch

A couple of days after stencilling a piece, paint it with two coats of protective clear varnish. Check on an inconspicuous area first to make sure that the paint does not run.

teapot stencil

Add a colourful touch to the kitchen with a teapot motif. Use the teapot as a border along the wall or to decorate cupboard doors.

A yellow border, consisting of a dotted line, was stencilled along the wall just above the tiles. The blue teapot motif was then added just above it.

If creating a border on a wall, as opposed to using the stencil on cupboard doors, measure the length of the wall. Work out how many times you can repeat the teapot along this length. If you are stencilling above a row of tiles, as here, you can centre the motif above every second tile if they are the standard 15cm / 6in square. In this case, do check where the motif will fall at the two ends of the border.

USE THE TEAPOT MOTIF • to create a border • on kitchen units • on cupboard doors • on containers.

Leave yourself enough room to stencil the teapot on the wall. If working above a work top, clear it to leave yourself some elbow space and cover it with newspapers to make cleaning up easier. Stencil the border first and leave it to dry before adding the teapot motif.

1 Measure the length of the surface and mark the centre point. Find the centre of the stencil and align it with the centre point of the wall.

2 Stencil the base border, masking off the lower part of the teapot before you start. Use the half square as the repeat mark when repositioning the stencil.

Craftytip

Use clear tape to mask off the border so you can see it when stencilling the teapot.

3 Cover the border cutouts on the stencil with masking tape. Stencil the first teapot motif in the centre.

4 Keeping the spacing even and following your measurements, continue stencilling the teapot.

final touch

You can stencil squares at random using a square or check stencil on the wall to create a sugar lump effect.

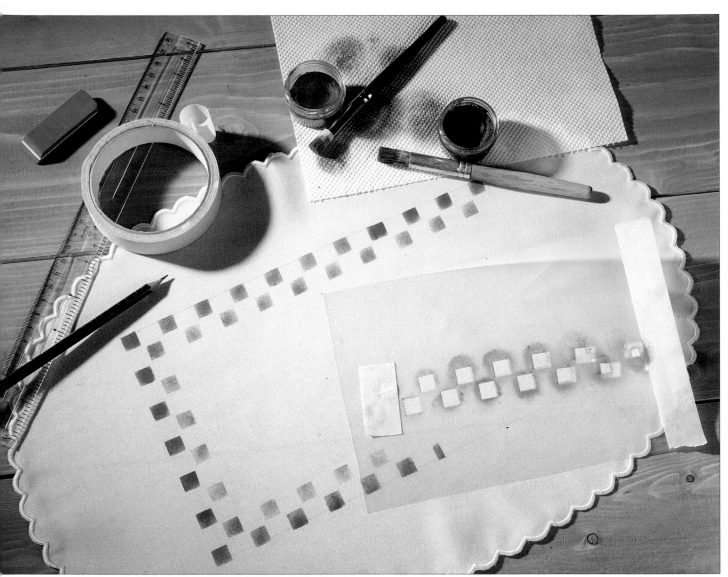

stencilling on *fabric*

This simple, stencilled check design will add an individual, decorative touch – choose colours that will brighten up your kitchen.

The most suitable fabrics for stencilling are cotton and linen, but silk and 50/50 cotton/polyester mixes can also be used. Avoid synthetic fibres, wool and heavy textured cloth as these are not suitable for this technique. Pre-wash the fabric and iron out any creases. When the stencilled fabric is dry, heat-seal it with an iron set to the appropriate temperature for the fabric. Stencilled fabric should be handwashed gently in cool, soapy water or, with a washing machine, using a programme for delicate fabrics.

USE STENCILS ON • napkins • blinds • curtains • placemats.

Geometric stencil designs must be positioned accurately, so work out where you want your design in advance and practise on a piece of scrap fabric. You can also experiment with different colours and designs. Always work on a flat surface that gives you plenty of elbow room.

Craftytip

Stencils can become clogged with paint, so clean them regularly as you work with absorbent kitchen roll.

Napkins and table mats can be stencilled with the same check design, but in contrasting colours.

1 Work out how many squares you want along the length and breadth of the pattern. Measure out the design carefully, marking the fabric lightly with a pencil or tailor's chalk.

2 Starting at the top left-hand corner, stencil the top row in one colour and the bottom row in a second colour. Use light strokes and do not overload the brushes with paint.

3 Finish the top row and place the stencil along the left-hand pencil line. Paint in the design to form a corner. Mask off those parts of the stencil that are not being used.

4 Place the stencil on the bottom line. Stencil along the line to form a second corner. Continue around the grid until the grid is completed. Leave overnight for the paint to dry before heat-sealing it with an iron.

punched tin
CABINET

Tin plate is easy to work. With a hammer and bradawl, you can make an attractive new front panel for a cabinet.

You can produce a variety of designs as simple or intricate as you like on pieces of tin. All that is involved is simply punching indentations on the metal with a hammer and bradawl.

The tin used for this design was specially cut to size by the hardware shop where it was bought, so it didn't need cutting out with tin snips. You can also experiment with the tops from tin cans and punch through a design in the same way to make Christmas tree decorations — keep them out of children's reach, though, as the edges will be sharp.

You will need

TAPE MEASURE OR RULER

TRACING PAPER AND PENCIL

MARKER PEN

TIN SNIPS

SMALL WOODEN CABINET

TIN OR ALUMINIUM

REPOSITIONABLE SPRAY ADHESIVE

THICK MAGAZINE OR CORK TILES

BRADAWL

HAMMER

PANEL PINS

chapter five

making a pinhole design

The centre panel of the cabinet was removed and replaced from the back with tin plate. If you have to cut the metal to size yourself, use a pair of tin snips.

Enlarge the pattern to the size you require and draw it on graph paper the same size as your panel.

1 Measure the front panel of your cabinet. Allow 15mm / ⅔in all round for fixing, if attaching from the back. Enlarge the template shown here to the size you require (see Enlarging a Design, p6), or draw out your own design on graph paper. You could also trace a favourite design and dot the lines at regular intervals.

2 Trace over the dots on to a sheet of tracing paper (A). If you use a thick marker pen, you will get a good sized dot when it comes to punching out the design.

A. Use a thick marker pen to trace over the dots on to a sheet of tracing paper.

3 Use tin snips to cut out a piece of tin or aluminium to the measurements worked out in Step One. Alternatively, get your hardware shop to cut the tin to size when you buy it.

4 Place your tracing paper over the piece of tin so that the design is centred. Attach the tracing paper firmly with spray adhesive.

5 Place a thick magazine or cork tiles under the tin. Position a bradawl vertically above the first dot of the design to be punched.

6 Tap the bradawl with a hammer through the tracing paper to the metal until you achieve the type of punch-hole effect you require (B). It is a good idea to do a test on an offcut first. The harder and the more times you tap, the deeper the hole will be. Tap through all the holes until the design is complete.

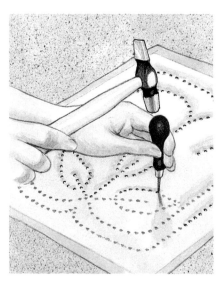

B. Gently tap the bradawl with a hammer through the tracing paper to make dents in the tin.

7 Carefully remove the centre panel of the cupboard door, by scoring the joins, easing out any nails and prising off the inner frame of wood. When there is an opening at the front, replace the inner frame with panel pins. Square up the punched tin design and attach it to the inside of the cabinet, tapping in panel pins at regular intervals (C).

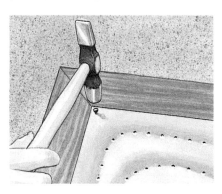

C. Use panel pins at regular intervals to attach the tin design to the cabinet.

ALTERNATIVE DESIGN

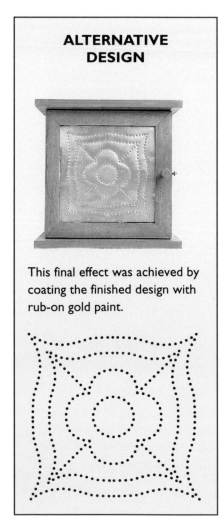

This final effect was achieved by coating the finished design with rub-on gold paint.

decorated TABLEWARE

Decorate any plain tableware in pretty colours with cold ceramic paints using masking fluid to create an original pattern.

Cold ceramic paints do not conform to food safety regulations and so should not be used on any items where they will come into contact with food or drink. They are, however, suitable for a variety of items made out of ceramic, for example, salt and pepper pots, vinaigrette containers, mustard pots and water jugs, where only the outside surfaces are painted, making their use perfectly safe.

If you want to use the paints on plates or mugs, the best way to ensure that these are safe is to decorate the object so that the painted areas won't come into contact with any food or drink. A plate should be only decorated with a border or frieze and a mug can be painted on the outside but leave about 2.5cm / 1in clear from the rim down.

You will need

PLAIN CERAMIC JUG

DETERGENT

MASKING FLUID

SMALL PAINTBRUSH

COLD CERAMIC PAINT IN RED, YELLOW, WHITE, AND GREEN

SCALPEL OR CRAFT KNIFE

painting tableware

Stick to a combination of wavy lines and circles to create a simple pattern on ceramic surfaces and use colours that complement your existing decor. Don't try anything too ambitious unless you are good at free-hand drawing.

1 Prepare the surface of the vinaigrette bottle by cleaning it with detergent to make sure it is free of any grease.

A. Paint on the masking fluid to create a pattern on the container.

2 Create a design on the container using masking fluid, following the instructions on the pot. Dots and wavy lines were used here. Divide the top and bottom of the container with a clear, wavy line. Paint the fluid on to the bottle with a fine paintbrush (A), applying it quite thickly. Leave for about 15-20 minutes until dry.

B. Apply the ceramic paint over the masked-out areas.

3 Paint the top half of the bottle (a vivid orange, made from mixing red and yellow with a little white paint, was used here). Decorate the handle (a single yellow line was used here) and then paint the lower half of the container with wide stripes (B), alternating two colours (green and yellow in this case). Leave the paint to dry.

C. Remove the dry masking fluid with a craft knife or scalpel.

The salt and pepper pots were decorated in the same way as the vinaigrette jug but using different colours.

4 Use a scalpel or craft knife to remove the masking fluid (C). To do this, catch one small part of the dried fluid with the blade of the knife and then pull it up and towards you. The dried fluid should pull off quite easily, like dried glue. Don't worry if it does not come off in one go as any remnants can be scraped away carefully.

WORK BOX

MASKING FLUID

Watercolour masking fluid is used to protect areas that are not to be painted. It is a mixture of rubber and latex, and when dry, peels off the ceramic surface rather like dry PVA glue. The advantage of using a fluid rather than stickers is that you can paint delicate patterns without being restricted to straight lines or circles. When not using the fluid, keep it in a safe place, away from children, as it is toxic.

You will need

FOR BASIC RECIPE:

100G / 4OZ PLAIN WHITE FLOUR

50G / 2OZ FINE TABLE SALT

10ML / 2TSP VEGETABLE OIL

60ML / 2½ FL OZ WATER

MIXING BOWL

ROLLING PIN

KNIFE

EGG AND WATER TO GLAZE

CLEAR VARNISH

working with
salt dough

Use everyday household ingredients to make anything from bread baskets to seasonal decorations with a touch of traditional cheer.

Creating objects out of such basic ingredients as salt, flour and water is an ancient craft. Salt dough modelling has given generations of bakers an opportunity to show off their technical skills by adorning their shops with elaborate baskets, wreaths and festival loaves.

USE SALT DOUGH FOR • making seasonal decorations • bowls and baskets • folk and fairytale figures • novelty animals • jewellery.

For ceramic-hard results, salt dough is dried out very slowly by baking in an oven for about six hours at 145°C/290°F or three hours at gas 1½. Glazing prevents the dough from taking up moisture. When the bread has cooled completely, seal it with a coat of clear varnish.

MAKING COILS

MAKING LATTICE-WORK

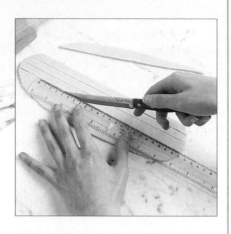

1 Using a rolling pin, roll out the salt dough until it is about 6mm / ¼in thick. Cut into strips 2cm / ¾in wide and place one strip across a wetted baking sheet. Lay the second strip over one end, at a right angle.

2 Keep laying more dough strips at right angles to each other, weaving them over and under the first and second strips. Continue in this way, lifting and replacing the strips as you add more until you have reached the end of the strips.

1 Roll the dough into two long sausages of equal length using the palms of your hands. Cross over the two sausages in the middle and twist them tightly but gently together, working away from the centre. Do not pull the dough as it will stretch and break.

2 To join the ends of the coils, trim them with a knife. Separate the four ends, and cut each one diagonally so that they match when joined. To secure, wet the dough with a little water and press the ends together to complete the coil.

MAKING SALT DOUGH

1 Stir the flour and salt together in a large mixing bowl. Add the oil and water and mix thoroughly.

2 Knead the ingredients into a ball, adding a little more water, if necessary.

3 Turn the dough on to a flat, floured work surface. Continue to knead for about 10 minutes until the ball of dough is smooth and silky.

final touch

Bake the dough until hard, glaze with an egg yolk mixed with 15ml / 1tbsp water. Bake for 30 minutes. When cool seal with clear varnish.

a lattice-work
BREAD BASKET

A lattice and coil salt-dough basket, glazed and varnished, will brighten up your breakfast table. Add some ears of wheat as a decorative touch and simply fill with oven-fresh rolls.

A pretty salt-dough basket filled with fragrant rolls is the perfect complement to a pot of freshly brewed coffee. Bread baskets have always been one of the traditional themes for salt dough, perhaps because the colours of bread and real wickerwork are so similar. They are also associated with the Harvest Festival, hence the salt-dough wheat-ear decoration.

Our basket is hard-wearing if treated with care. It has been designed for bread but you could fill it with fruit or vegetables and make it a feature of your kitchen decor.

You will need

1.1 LITRE / 2 PT PIE DISH

2 BAKING TRAYS

ALUMINIUM FOIL

SALT DOUGH

FOUR TIMES BASIC RECIPE, SEE SALT DOUGH TECHNIQUE P 1

ROLLING PIN

KNIFE AND FORK OR SKEWER

SMALL PASTRY BRUSH

FOR GLAZING: 2 EGG YOLKS MIXED WITH 30ML / 2 TBSP WATER

CLEAR VARNISH

FAST-BONDING GLUE

making the basket

This pretty bread basket is easy to make and very decorative. It uses both the coiling and lattice salt-dough techniques.

1 Place the deep pie dish, base upwards, on a damp baking tray. Cover the dish with kitchen foil.

2 Roll out two lengths of salt dough, each about 25cm / 10in longer than the circumference of the dish itself. Put the remainder in a plastic bag to prevent it from drying out.

3 To make a coil, twist the two lengths of dough together (see p98) and arrange it around the rim of the dish. Trim the ends neatly with a knife so that opposite ends butt up against each other. Moisten the ends and join them together (A).

4 Roll out the rest of the salt dough and cut it into thin strips about 1.2cm / ½in wide and long enough to go over the dish. Weave the lattice (see p98) over the dish (B).

5 Wherever the dough crosses over dough, brush with a little water. To finish, trim the ends neatly with a knife. Brush the undersides with water and join them to the rim, piercing with a fork or skewer to secure the strips to the coil (C). Place another baking tray on top of the pastry-covered dish and press down firmly. This will ensure that the bread basket lies flat when in use.

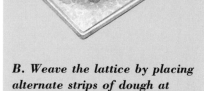

A. Make a tight coil of salt dough around the rim of the upturned dish.

B. Weave the lattice by placing alternate strips of dough at right angles to each other.

C. Secure the strips to the coil by piercing them with a fork or skewer into the coil.

6 Place the basket in the oven and bake it for six hours at 145°C / 290°F or three hours at gas 1½. Tap the dough lightly at the end of the cooking time to check that it is hard. The dough should sound hollow if it is ready. If it sounds dull, bake it for a further 30 minutes. Glaze the outside with the egg mixture and bake for a further 30 minutes. Remove the basket carefully from the pie dish. Turn it the right way up and glaze the inside. Bake it for a further 30 minutes.

7 Turn the oven off, leaving the basket inside to cool. When the basket is completely cold, remove it from the oven and seal it with a couple of coats of clear varnish.

final touch

To decorate the basket with ears of wheat, roll small lumps of dough into almond shapes – you will need about 25. Snip diagonally up each shape. Bake the ears and allow them to cool. Attach the ears to the basket rim with fast-bonding glue, before painting with varnish to seal.

country kitchen
CLOCK

Turn a ready-made frame into a harvest clock by decorating it with seeds and flowers, and adding a battery-operated mechanism.

You don't have to be a Swiss watchmaker to create your own original timepiece. The battery-operated clock mechanism is available from hobby shops and by mail order. All you do is attach it to a framed plywood background and decorate it as you please.

The clock is set in a ready-made frame sectioned off with balsa wood, available from hobby shops. It is very easy to cut – you don't need a saw, a craft knife will do the job. The balsa wood sections are decorated with pasta, whole spices, pulses (lentils were used for the clock-face numbers), coffee beans and dried flowers.

You can adapt the clock if you like. For example, for a children's room, paint it in bright colours and use sweets on the clock face.

You will need

WOODEN PICTURE FRAME, ABOUT 27 x 33CM / 10 ½ x 13IN

4MM PLYWOOD THE SAME SIZE AS THE FRAME

MEDIUM-GRADE SANDPAPER

13MM / ½IN PANEL PINS

HAMMER

WOOD STAIN TO MATCH FRAME

SMALL PAINTBRUSH

SCISSORS

BLANK PAPER

PENCIL AND RULER

CARBON PAPER

DRILL AND DRILL BIT

CRAFT KNIFE

6MM / ¼IN SQUARE BALSA WOOD STRIP, 90CM / 3FT LONG

ALL-PURPOSE CLEAR ADHESIVE

SELECTION OF SEEDS, WHOLE SPICES, PASTA SHAPES AND DRIED FLOWERS

BATTERY-OPERATED CLOCK MECHANISM AND HANDS

2 x 25MM / 1IN CUP HOOKS

PICTURE WIRE

making the kitchen clock

The size of the hole required for the clock depends on the type of mechanism being used. Check with the instructions that come with it and use the appropriate-sized drill bit.

1 Discard the glass and backing from the frame. Smooth the edges of the plywood with sandpaper if necessary. Nail the plywood to the back of the frame using the panel pins. Brush the wood stain on the front of the plywood and leave to dry.

2 Cut a piece of paper to fit inside the frame. Work out your design on this, using the template below as a guide. To enlarge the template, see Enlarging a Design, p6.

3 Transfer your design on to the plywood background using carbon paper. Drill a hole at the mark in the centre of the clock face and smooth the edges of the hole with sandpaper.

4 Use a craft knife to cut the balsa wood according to your design. Arrange the balsa wood on the template. Decide what you are putting in each section and write the details on the template. Apply wood stain to the balsa and leave to dry.

5 Glue the balsa wood to the background, according to your design. Fill the sections with pasta, seeds or your chosen decorations, gluing them in position as you go. Add hour marks to the clock face.

Details of the clock, showing the clock face, balsa wood sections, ready-made frame, plywood backing and clock mechanism.

6 Insert the clock mechanism through the plywood, according to the manufacturer's instructions.

7 To hang the clock, screw cup hooks into the back of the frame and attach picture wire across them.

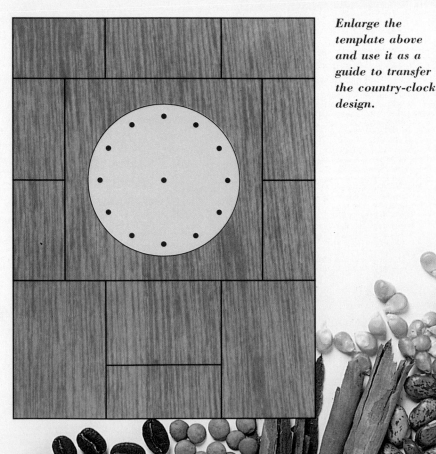

Enlarge the template above and use it as a guide to transfer the country-clock design.

painted CUTLERY HOLDER

Mix a little colour pigment with an egg yolk to make paint and use it to decorate a plain cutlery box with a folk-art appeal.

A ready-made softwood box, available from most pine shops and the kitchen departments of large stores, was used for this paint project although you can make your own if you wish – for full details, see overleaf. Use offcuts of softwood and cut the pieces out using a jigsaw.

The pattern is applied freehand so keep it simple. Don't try anything too elaborate or you'll lose the naive charm of the decoration. The pigments are available from arts and crafts shops and come in a range of colours. Always follow the manufacturer's instructions, particularly if using toxic pigments (powdered poster colours can be used instead). To make the paint more hardwearing, apply two or three coats of clear polyurethane varnish to the finished box.

You will need

PALE BLUE, RED AND YELLOW COLOUR PIGMENTS

TEASPOON

OLD SAUCERS OR SMALL SAUCEPAN

SOFT ARTIST'S PAINTBRUSHES

PLAIN SOFTWOOD CUTLERY BOX (TO MAKE YOUR OWN, SEE OVERLEAF)

CLEAR MATT POLYURETHANE VARNISH

painting the cutlery holder

Smooth the box with fine grade sandpaper, as necessary. Mix the paints as you need them and use them straight away. Paint the background colour first and leave it to dry before adding the pattern. When mixing colours to make new ones, mix the pigments together before combining them with the egg yolk.

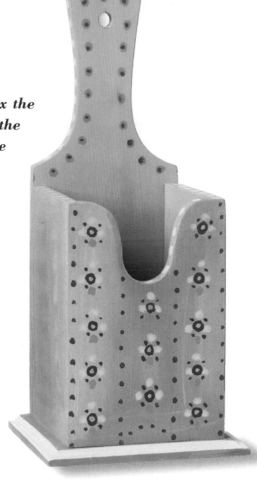

1 To make the paint, remove the membrane from the yolk and discard it. Place the yolk in an old saucer. Place a little colour pigment next to the yolk and press it with the back of the spoon to remove any lumps. Work the pigment in to the yolk to make a paste, adding a little water to make a paint with a creamy consistency.

2 To paint the inside of the box, mix blue and yellow pigment to make green then add more

yellow to get the right shade. Paint the whole of the inside of the box. Leave to dry.

3 Make up a pale blue paint and paint the outside. Leave the back unpainted if you wish.

4 Mix paints for the patterns, and decorate the box. Paint the strip around the base yellow. Leave the paint to dry. Apply two coats of varnish, leaving it to dry between coats.

TO MAKE THE BOX

To make your own box, use 12mm / ½in planed softwood. Assemble the pieces with wood glue and moulding pins before decorating it.

1 Cut the pieces following the cutting plan. Round the top edge of three sides of the base with sandpaper and drill a hole in the back as indicated.

2 Apply wood glue to the edges and assemble the box, keeping the edges aligned. Wrap masking tape around the box to keep it in place while it dries.

3 To secure the box permanently, lay it on its front and use moulding pins and a hammer to pin the back along the outside edges to the sides, keeping the spacing even. Turn the box over and secure the front to the side pieces in the same way. Use a metal punch to sink the nail heads just below the surface of the wood.

4 Use a little wall or wood filler to fill the nail holes and any gaps along the edges. Leave to dry then smooth the surface down with fine grade sandpaper. Decorate the box as above.

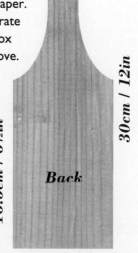

Sides x 2

16.5cm / 6½in

9cm / 3½in

Base

12cm / 4¾in

Front

14cm / 5½in

11cm / 4⅜in

Back

30cm / 12in

16.5cm / 6½in

11cm / 4⅜in

tie-on covered
SEAT PAD

Add a soft touch and some colour to kitchen chairs with seat pads made out of foam and covered with bright fabrics.

You can buy pieces of foam for the seat pads from department stores or market stalls. If you can't find the right shape, then buy a sheet of 2.5cm / 1in foam, make a template of the chair seat and use it to cut out the required foam shape. The seat pads are attached to the chairs with self-ties. Check that these are positioned to match up to the struts on the chairs.

The piped cushion is reversible. You can finish the back opening with a zip, Velcro or poppers to make it easy to remove the cover for washing.

An alternative design features a jagged edge, made from triangles of fabric sewn into the seam. This can be turned into a fun finish by using plain bright fabric for the cover and alternating two or three contrasting plain colours for the triangles.

You will need

FOR EACH CUSHION:

CUSHION PAD OR FOAM

50CM / 20IN EACH OF TWO CONTRASTING FABRICS, FOR REVERSIBLE COVER

1M / 40IN OF FABRIC FOR THE NOVELTY CUSHION

SCRAPS OF CONTRASTING FABRICS

TAILOR'S CHALK

SCISSORS

1M / 40IN PIPING CORD

1M / 40IN BIAS BINDING

PINS, SEWING NEEDLE AND THREAD

SEWING MACHINE

POPPERS, VELCRO OR ZIP

making the covered seat pad

If you are using a fabric with a dominant design or stripe, try to centre this on the cushion when cutting out the fabric. Cut the foam pad to shape if necessary.

SEAT WITH TRIANGULAR FRINGE

1 Cut two pieces of fabric for the cover, using the pad as a guide. Cut several small squares, 6x6cm / 2¼x2¼in, in the main fabric and contrasting fabric. Place matching squares right sides together and cut the diagonals to form triangles.

2 Taking a narrow seam allowance, sew the two short sides of each triangle. Trim across the point close to the stitching and turn to right side (A).

A. Sew the two short sides and trim the points.

3 Alternating plain and patterned triangles, arrange them on the right side of one fabric piece, with the points facing inwards and the raw edges to the outside. The ends of the triangles need to overlap a little otherwise there will be a gap between them when the cushion is turned through.

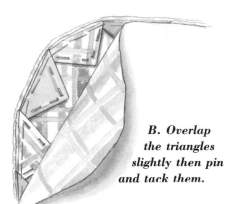

B. Overlap the triangles slightly then pin and tack them.

4 Pin and tack the triangles (B). Machine stitch them in place. Place the cover pieces right sides together, sandwiching the triangles, and stitch again, within the first stitching line.

5 Trim the seam allowances, clip the curves and turn the cover to the right side. Finish the back opening with poppers, a zip or Velcro. Insert the foam pad.

6 Cut two strips of fabric, 45x5cm / 18x2in. Fold in half along the length and stitch a narrow seam, forming a tube. Turn the tubes through and hand sew the ends to close. Check the position of the ties against the chair and sew the centre of each tie in position to the back straight edge.

The ties are attached to the back edge of the cover.

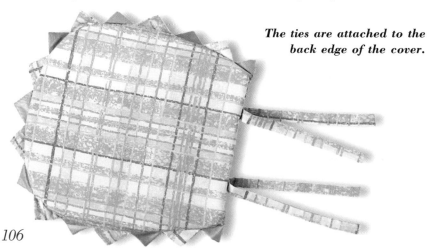

REVERSIBLE PIPED SEAT

1 Lay the cushion pad on the wrong side of one piece of fabric and use tailor's chalk to draw all around it, adding on a 2.5cm / 1in seam allowance on the curved edge and 4cm / 1½in extra at the back straight edge. Repeat with the other piece of fabric and cut out.

2 Cover the piping cord with blue bias binding. Pin, tack and stitch the cord around the curved edge on the right side of one cushion piece with the raw edges together.

C. Place fabric right sides together and sandwich the piping inside.

3 Lay the other cushion piece over this, right sides together, and pin, tack and machine stitch around three sides, close to the piping cord and leaving the straight seam open (C). Trim the seam, clip the curves, press and turn through.

4 Turn in the seam allowance at the back straight edge and close with poppers, a zip or Velcro. Insert the foam pad.

5 Cut two strips of each fabric, 45x5cm / 18x2in. Place right sides together and stitch along the long edges taking narrow seams. Turn through to right sides and stitch ends by hand.

6 Check the position of the ties against the chair and sew the centre of each tie in position to the back straight edge.

making roller blinds

You can use stiffened roller blind fabric or choose a suitable fabric and stiffen it yourself with spray-on stiffener to make blinds.

Roller blinds are one of the quickest and most economical methods of covering a window, yet people are often a little nervous of making them. The secret lies in choosing the right fabric, and in ensuring it is cut square and attached square to the roller.

Use a ready-stiffened fabric designed for roller blinds, or stiffen your own fabric using a spray-on stiffener. If using spray-on stiffener, it's wise to cut the fabric a little wider and longer than required in case of shrinkage – the excess can be trimmed away later.

Stitch a casing across the lower edge of the fabric to hold a wooden lath to create a firm edge – the acorn used to pull the blind up and let it down is screwed into this lath. Use a double-sided tape to help you secure the blind to the roller while you hammer in the tacks, spacing them evenly.

Attach the brackets in place before you start so that you can measure the fabric accordingly.

USE ROLLER BLINDS • in the kitchen • in the bathroom • instead of lace curtains • where curtains are purely decorative and don't cover the window completely.

*S*et the brackets on either side of the window, with the round hole bracket to the right. Screw in place. Measure the distance between the brackets to find the width of the blind, making allowances for the shoulders of the pins on the roller.

1 Measure the roller from the shoulder at the flat pin end and cut the wood to length. Place the cap over the cut end. Use a bradawl to make a hole in the centre and hammer in the round pin, being careful not to rest on and damage the flat pin.

2 Set the fabric on a work surface, right side up, and measure out the correct depth, allowing 25cm / 10in extra for the hem and the roller wraparound. Mark out and cut using a set square to ensure a square top edge.

3 Fold 6cm / 2¼in of the blind fabric to the wrong side, then fold over a further 5cm / 2in, smoothing the fold down well with your fingers to make a neat crease. Machine stitch along the edge of the hem to form a pocket for the lath.

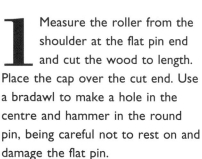

4 Place the roller across the wrong side of the fabric 3cm / 1¼in in from the edge, with the flat pin to the right. Attach the top edge of the material to the roller using double-sided tape, then hammer in the tacks provided with the roller.

5 Cut the lath to the length required and insert it into the casing at the lower edge of the blind. Measure the width of the blind to find the centre of the lower edge. Screw in the attachment for the string and acorn pull to the front.

HANGING THE BLIND

The blind needs to be tensioned to the required spring to go up and down. Roll up the blind, ensuring it is even, then hang the blind. Pull the blind down, remove it from the brackets and roll it up again to half-way. Hang the blind again and pull it down. Test by pulling the blind – it should roll up to the top. If not, take it down, reroll and repeat the process.

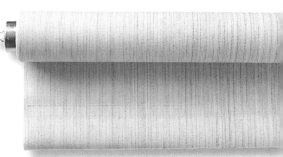

limed wood

You will need

FINE GRADE STEEL WOOL

LIMING WAX

SOFT CLOTHS

FINISHING WAX
(FURNITURE POLISH)

Liming wax works best on oak, a wood with which it is traditionally associated. But, as the example here shows, any coarse, open-grained timber can be used to good effect. The resulting pale finish can be further decorated.

Traditionally used to preserve wood, liming is now more often used as a decorative finish. Apart from preserving wood, it also whitens it, leaving an attractive pale finish. Lime, a calcium compound, was originally used for the technique and was mainly done by professionals as handling lime can be hazardous. As its finish is still much admired, ways have been found of achieving the same effect without using the lime in its original form: nowadays, safer preservatives have taken over.

The technique given here uses liming wax and is without the dangers associated with the real thing. Not so much a preservative as a decorative device, liming provides an excellent background for stencilling. It can also be coloured with emulsion paint. To do this the wood is given a wash of emulsion paint diluted with water. The water evaporates leaving the colour pigment behind. The liming wax is then applied over this. Liming wax is available from hardware stores and decorator's suppliers as well as some arts and crafts shops.

USE LIMING WAX • for a decorative finish • to give a bleached look.

Liming wax works best on untreated surfaces. If the surface has been polished, painted or varnished, the wood must be stripped first if results are to be successful. If a coloured finish is required, apply this first. Use wax furniture polish, not a spray-on one, for the final finish.

1 Using the steel wool, apply a generous amount of liming wax to the wood, rubbing it well into the grain. Leave for 5-10 minutes to dry.

2 Remove any excess liming wax with a soft cloth and furniture wax. Change to a clean cloth as the last one becomes saturated with liming wax.

3 Keep rubbing until the liming wax has settled into the grain of the wood and you are left with a soft sheen.

Craftytip

To colour the wood, use a wash of emulsion paint diluted with water. Brush it all over the piece and leave it to dry before liming the surface.

THE
BEDROOM

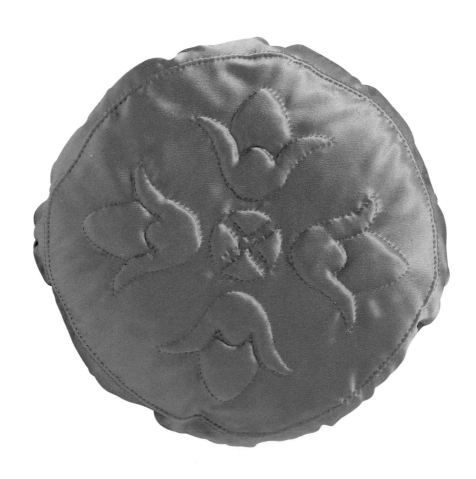

The Bedroom

CONTENTS

quilt-as-you-go log cabin

This technique has much to commend it, as blocks are quilted individually before joining them in pairs, then in rows.

This is a quick method of working the traditional log cabin design or block, using a sewing machine, in which you piece the block and quilt the design all in one go. The blocks are sewn directly on to individual squares of fabric and wadding (a white backing is used here for clarity, but a colour or pattern would be better). Each block is formed around a patterned square of fabric, around which strips of fabric in two other colours are sewn in a specific sequence.

The completed blocks are then joined in pairs, then rows, which transforms the design – the squares cease to be the focus as the yellow strips lie adjacent to each other to form a kind of diamond shape.

Choose pure cotton fabric, in plain colours or in small prints. Keep seam allowances consistent, or use the sewing machine foot as a guide, if suitable.

USE THIS TECHNIQUE • to make bed quilts • for wall hangings.

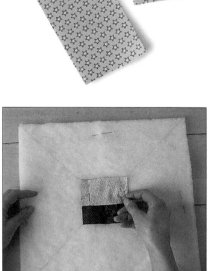

*F*or complete accuracy, make a few trial pieces, then carefully check the measurements before starting to work. Cut four 33cm / 13in squares in the backing fabric and the wadding, four 9cm / 3½in squares of green spotted fabric, and six 5cm / 2in wide strips from each of the yellow and blue fabrics.

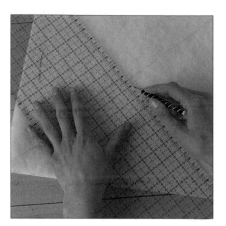

1 Pin the wadding over the backing squares and using a ruler and a soft pencil, draw two diagonal lines from corner to corner, forming a cross.

2 Pin the green spotted square to the centre, matching the four corners, so that they touch the pencil cross.

3 Cut a length from the yellow strip, the same size as the square, and place over the top edge of the square, right sides together. Pin as shown.

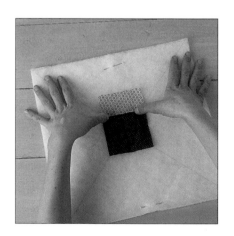

4 Sew through all thicknesses using the edge of the machine foot as a guide for seam allowances. Take out the pins and finger press the strip upwards. Give the work a quarter turn anticlockwise.

Craftytip

To avoid unsightly thread tangles on the back, hold the top thread taut at the back of the foot as the first stitch is made. Work a double stitch at the beginning and the end of the row, by operating the reverse button on the sewing machine.

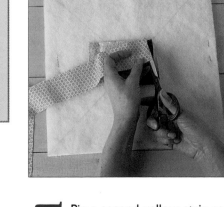

5 Pin a second yellow strip as before, fold back the strip and finger press it so that the strip is level with the side of the square. Cut along this fold.

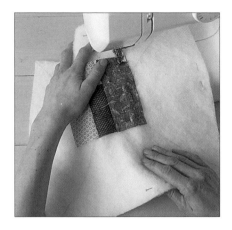

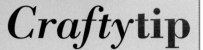

Craftytip

It's advisable to pin the longer strips flat after they have been pressed back, before working the final round.

6 Pin and sew, then take out the pins and finger press upwards. Turn the work anticlockwise. Take a blue strip, pin right sides together along the top square, including the yellow strip, fold back and trim. Pin and sew the piece as before.

7 Fold the strip upwards and finger press. Turn the work anticlockwise. Work the final side of the square so it is now surrounded by two yellow and two blue strips. The corners should be touching the pencil cross.

8 Continue building up the strips in the same way until two rounds of each colour are in place. Sew the first yellow strip as before.

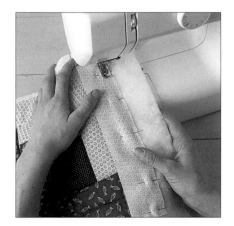

9 Start sewing the second yellow strip, 2.5cm / 1in in from the beginning.

10 Start the first blue strip 2.5cm / 1in from the beginning, then add the second blue strip, finishing the stitching 2.5cm / 1in from the end (the ends must be detached from the wadding).

11 Sew the detached ends by hand with a small running stitch.

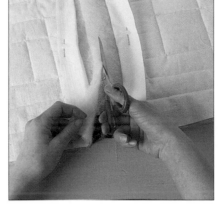

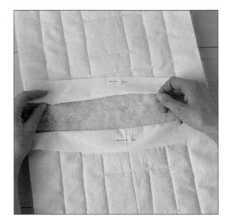

12 Place the blocks in pairs, right sides and yellow strips together, then in a group of four, to form a yellow diamond in the centre. Pin back the wadding and backing fabric, and pin the edges of the yellow strips together.

13 Machine stitch, then finger press the seam allowances open. Open the pairs of blocks flat, overlap the edges of the wadding and cut down the centre so the edges butt up.

14 Sew together, using a herringbone stitch, keeping the join flat and taking care not to catch the fabric underneath.

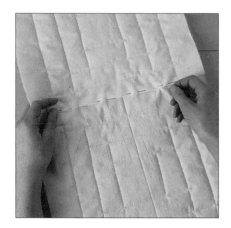

15 Working from the back, fold in a seam allowance, centring over the seam on the front by pushing a pin through as a guide. Slip stitch, sewing through the wadding, but not the front fabric except for the first and last 2.5cm / 1in of the seam. Join these two pairs, in the same way as above, making four blocks.

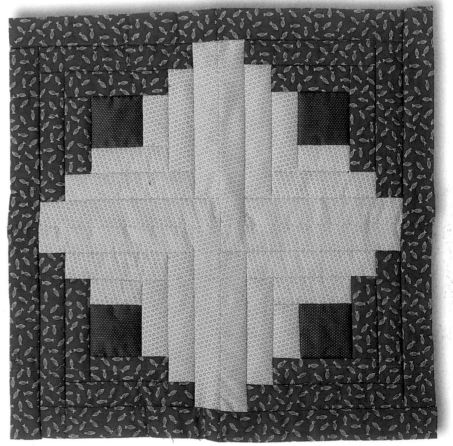

wardrobe MAKEOVER

A battered second-hand wardrobe is given a new lease of life with this easy-to-apply, paint-over-wax technique.

This wardrobe was completely transformed from a dreary brown to a colourful green using the technique of wipe-away paint on wax. This is a finish that can be used to great effect on any worn wooden surface, and is a highly successful way of transforming dull pieces of furniture. Preparation is all-important – old varnish and any dirt must be removed before doing the makeover.

A base coat of matt emulsion – in a light colour – is applied, followed by a second coat of two colours of a similar tone. When dry, furniture wax is applied. A final coat in a different colour, in this case dark green, is painted on over the wax and left to dry, then gently sanded to provide the distressed effect.

You will need

PACK OF MEDIUM SANDPAPER

OLD WARDROBE

MATT EMULSION IN TWO LIGHT COLOURS AND ONE IN A DARKER COLOUR

PAINTBRUSHES

WAX FURNITURE POLISH

VARNISH (OPTIONAL)

GOLD PAINT OR GOLD LEAF

MASKING TAPE

decorating the wardrobe

Don't worry if your wardrobe is chipped or cracked – any defects will blend into the overall finish. If the paint won't take, apply a primer or undercoat. Mask off the mirror while decorating the wardrobe.

1 Sand down the wardrobe with medium sandpaper. All the old varnish and dirt must be removed.

2 Apply a base coat of matt emulsion in a light colour (off-white in this case).

3 Leave to dry and sand lightly with medium sandpaper. Apply a coat of matt emulsion (green) and, while still wet, apply a second coat in a similar tone (yellow).

4 When dry, apply the furniture wax with a soft rag. Paint on a top coat of matt emulsion (mid-green) and leave to dry.

5 Sand with medium grade sandpaper, following the grain. The sandpaper clogs up quickly, so use small pieces of sandpaper wrapped around a block of wood and not a sanding block.

6 Paint the borders in dark green (A). Finish off with the gold detail (B), using either paint or gold leaf. Leave to dry. Apply two coats of varnish (this is optional) to protect the surface.

Craftytip

You can rub the surface with a wax candle instead of using the wax furniture polish.

B. Paint the decorative detail gold.

A. Highlight the borders with a coat of dark green paint.

coordinated BED LINEN

Re-vamp your bedroom decor and save money by making your own duvet cover and pillowcase.

You will need

4.5M / 5YD CHECK FABRIC, 140CM / 55IN WIDE

1M / 40IN PLAIN FABRIC, 140CM / 55IN WIDE

EIGHT 2.5CM / 1IN DIAMETER BUTTONS

FIVE 1.5CM / ½IN DIAMETER BUTTONS

SEWING THREAD

2M / 80IN PIPING CORD

2M / 80IN CONTRASTING BIAS BINDING

This duvet cover and pillowcase feature a plain flap which buttons up over the top of the striking green checked fabric that has a distinctly masculine feel. The combination of plain and pattern is a stylish one and is easily adapted to something more feminine. Instead of the green check, choose a small floral print and set it off with a coordinating plain fabric. Both pillowcase and duvet are made in the same way, with piping binding the edge of the overlapping plain flap which serves as the opening to insert the pillow or duvet.

The flap on the pillow is proportionally narrower than the duvet so the buttons won't get tangled in long hair or irritate the sleeper.

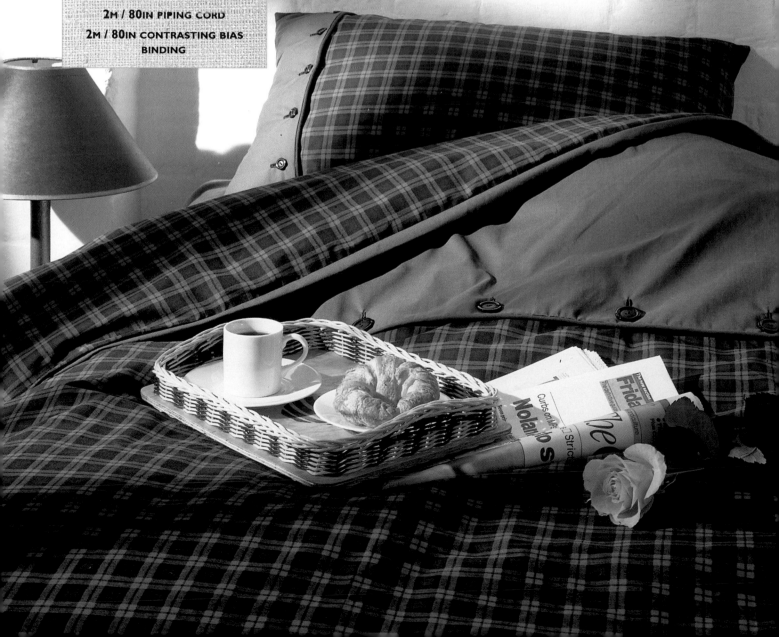

chapter six

making the bed linen

Instead of using check fabric, you can make the duvet cover and pillowcase using a combination of stripes and plain fabric, printed and plain fabric, or two contrasting shades of a plain fabric.

A. Place the narrow strip over the piping, right sides together.

B. Attach the flap to the back, right sides together.

C. Sew the front to the back.

THE PILLOWCASE

Finished size: 70x45cm / 27½x18in

1 Cut a piece of check fabric 74x49cm / 29x19in for the back and another piece 65x49cm / 25½x19in for the front. Cut a piece of plain fabric 25x49cm / 10x19in for the front. Cut a second plain strip measuring 15x49cm / 6x19in and neaten one long edge of the narrow strip with a small hem.

2 Cover a 49cm / 19in length of piping cord with navy bias binding. Sew covered cord to the long edge of the larger plain piece, right sides and raw edges together.

3 Lay the narrow hemmed strip over the piped edge, right sides and raw edges together (A). Stitch on the wrong side and trim the seam. Press the strip back so that the piping forms the edge.

4 Sew the contrasting strip to the back, right sides together, sewing round three sides of the contrasting strip and taking 2.5cm / 1in seams (B).

5 Fold a hem to the wrong side of the top of the front. Pin front to back, right sides together. Ensure the contrasting flap is correctly positioned. Stitch three sides, taking 2.5cm / 1in seams and leave the fourth side open (C). Trim the seams, clip the corners, turn to the right side and press.

6 Space the smaller buttons along the edge of the contrasting flap and mark their positions with chalk. Cut the buttonholes to size and stitch them in a contrasting thread. Attach the buttons in place to correspond with the buttonholes.

THE DUVET COVER

Finished size: 190x130cm / 75x51½in (single)

1 Cut a rectangle of checked fabric 195x135cm / 77x53½in for the back. Cut a checked rectangle 155x135cm / 61x53½in for the front. Cut a strip of plain fabric measuring 65x135cm / 25½x53½in.

2 Cut another strip from the plain fabric measuring 15x135cm / 6x53½in. Sew a hem along one edge of the length of the fabric to neaten it.

3 Cover a 135cm / 53½in length of piping cord with navy bias binding. Lay the piping cord over one long raw edge of the larger plain strip, raw edges together. Machine in place. To make up the duvet cover see Steps 3-5, above.

4 Space the larger buttons along the edge of the flap 2cm / ¾in in. Mark their positions. Check the flap overlaps the front and cut buttonholes to size. Stitch the holes in navy thread. Sew the buttons to the front beneath the flap to correspond with the buttonholes.

a heavenly
LAMPSHADE

Sometimes the simplest ideas are the most effective. By pricking a design into a paper lampshade it creates a sparkling pattern that lets the light shine through.

You will need

PENCIL

TRACING PAPER

MASKING TAPE

CARD
OR THIN CARTRIDGE PAPER

HATPIN

SCISSORS

FABRIC TAPE MEASURE

PAPER LAMPSHADE

LAMP BASE

THIMBLE
OPTIONAL

Stars are the perfect inspiration for a pinhole lampshade as they twinkle like the real thing. The clusters of small holes light up when you turn the lamp on and create a galaxy of illuminated patterns.

The designs are given overleaf for you to trace. Otherwise work out your own on a piece of graph paper – a grid helps to create symmetrical shapes. Remember that the dots need to be about 3mm / $\frac{1}{8}$in apart, depending on the thickness of the hatpin, otherwise the shade may tear when piercing it. You can use different sizes and shapes such as hearts, squares, triangles and diamonds.

making the lampshade

Work on the outside of the lampshade, piercing the holes towards the inside.

1 Trace the stars using the pattern provided, leaving a 2cm / ¾ in border around each design. Stick the designs down on to a piece of thick card with masking tape. Using the hatpin, pierce your designs through the two layers. Remove the tape and the tracing paper and cut out each pattern to provide a template. Label them A, B and C.

2 Measure the circumference at the base of the shade, starting from the seam (the one shown measured 109cm / 43in). Different-sized shades will alter the scale of the pattern by making the stars closer or farther apart.

3 Divide the measurement in half and mark it in pencil on the inside of the shade. Keep dividing your shade to create eight sections. Next, measure the top of the shade, then sub-divide this into four, marking each section.

4 Place template A on the outside of shade on the seam (see diagram below). Tape it down on the edge. Support the shade at the back and hold template (wear a thimble if you need to) so you can prick the shade without injuring yourself. Using the hatpin, pierce the pattern from the outside in. Repeat on the three other marks for A. Take template B and pierce the four stars around the top and in the gaps between the largest stars around the base. Finally, use template C and pierce stars as marked on the shade.

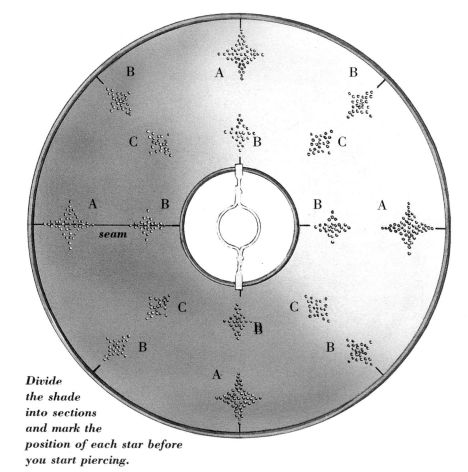

Divide the shade into sections and mark the position of each star before you start piercing.

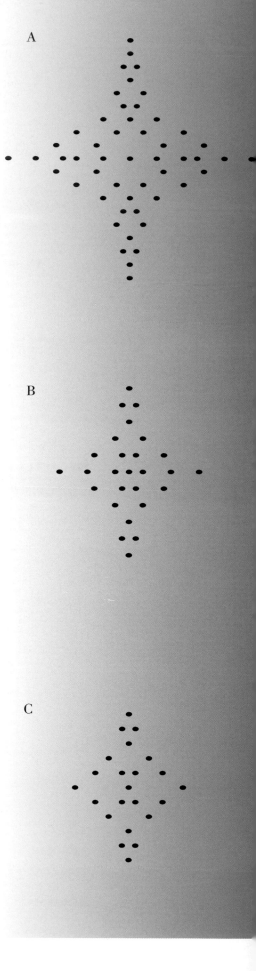

A

B

C

ribbon-edged
CURTAINS

A cased curtain is given a decorative edge to add colour and a touch of style.

Suitable for any room where you want a decorative finish, this cased curtain (where both curtains are hung right across the window, then draped to opposite sides) has a distinctive trim, made from folded ribbon edging with pearl drops.

The edging is applied to one edge of the front and the back lengths, so that it falls along the centre of the finished curtain. The edging is folded from broad ribbon to give a double-sided triangular effect. The finished appearance is a series of broad and narrow triangles studded with pearl drops. The pearl drops are sewn on individually by hand once the folded ribbon is stitched to the curtain. Use tiebacks to drape the curtains.

You will need

FOR A WINDOW WITH A 120CM/47IN DROP, 90CM/36IN WIDE:

3M/120IN FABRIC, 132 CM/52IN WIDE

9M/10YD CREAM RIBBON, 4CM/1½ IN WIDE

TAPE MEASURE

SCISSORS

SEWING MACHINE

30 PEARL DROPS

CREAM THREAD

SEWING NEEDLE

IRON

ADJUSTABLE BRASS CURTAIN ROD AND BRACKETS

making the edged curtain

Choose a fabric with no obvious right and wrong side. Instead of pearl drops, you can use beads. If you are making up a pair of cased curtains for two windows on the same wall, make up the pair as mirror images so that the top curtain of each one works as a pair over the two windows.

1 Hem both ends of the length of fabric, then fold it in half, aligning the two hems carefully. Stitch the casing with two lines of stitching, but don't thread the brass rod through at this point.

2 Holding one end of the length of ribbon, fold the short end over the width to the opposite side at an angle of 90° so the outside edge forms a diagonal and the inside edge is square (A).

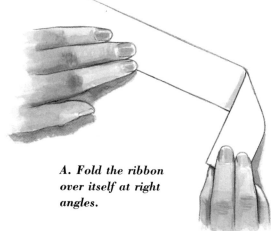

A. Fold the ribbon over itself at right angles.

3 Fold the remaining ribbon down along the folded edge to form a triangle.

4 Bring the free length up and repeat the process to form a reverse triangle (B). Repeat the sequence, forming a long strip with 'up and down' triangles and all the folds appearing on one side. Press to hold the folds in place.

5 Hand-stitch the ribbon edge to the right-hand edge of the top curtain and the left-hand edge of the bottom curtain so the edging is in the centre when the curtain is pulled back. Check that the hems are positioned correctly. Use a simple stab stitch, sewing down through the centre of the ribbon strip, with the wrong side of the ribbon strip facing upwards (C).

6 Press the ribbon edging towards the outer edge using an iron. Sew a pearl drop between each of the uppermost triangles. Thread the curtain on to the rod and hang as required with tiebacks.

B. Keep folding the ribbon over itself, aligning the edges exactly, to form a zigzag shape.

Craftytip

Use the same ribbon to make matching tiebacks for the curtain. Tie them into neat bows and decorate these with a few more pearl drops.

C. Sew the folded ribbon edge to the curtain by hand.

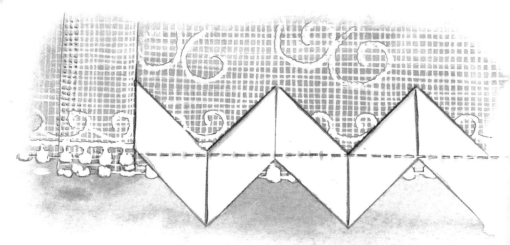

round
SILK CUSHION

A combination of Italian and trapunto quilting makes the perfect decoration for a silk cushion.

Silk satin is one of the most glamorous fabrics and this eye-catching cushion features both trapunto and Italian quilting, which show the fabric at its best. Use trapunto to work the central floral design and Italian to produce the corded effect around the edge. Use silk thread to work the quilting.

Satin catches the light and the raised areas formed by quilting two layers of fabric (silk and muslin) and inserting wadding from the back to enhance the effect. Use a quilting or embroidery frame to hold the design as you work to prevent the layers slipping. Use a cotton fabric for the backing.

You will need

- TRACING PAPER AND PENCIL
- MASKING TAPE
- SCISSORS
- DRESSMAKER'S CARBON AND TRACING WHEEL
- 40CM / ½YD SILK OR SOFT SATIN POLYESTER 114CM / 45IN WIDE
- 40CM / 15IN SQUARE OF MUSLIN OR MULL BACKING
- 40CM / 15IN SQUARE OF COTTON FABRIC
- QUILTING OR EMBROIDERY FRAME
- SILK THREAD AND SEWING NEEDLE
- 150CM / 59IN QUILTING WOOL
- HEAVY-DUTY OR TAPESTRY NEEDLE
- CROCHET HOOK
- TEASED-OUT WADDING OR SOFT TOY STUFFING
- SEWING MACHINE
- 25CM / 10IN ZIP
- 36CM / 14IN CIRCULAR CUSHION PAD

making the silk cushion

Italian (corded) and trapunto (stuffed) quilting use two layers of fabric only. Wadding and wool are added separately, after the motifs have been hand sewn.

1 Enlarge the design to measure 35.5cm / 14in in diameter (see Enlarging a Design, p6). Next cut a piece of silk 40cm / 16in square, and holding the silk flat with masking tape, trace the design centrally on to the right side using dressmaker's carbon paper and a tracing wheel.

2 Place the silk over the muslin square and grid tack the two layers together, using silk thread.

3 Stitch the motifs and the double circle. Remove the tacking, insert the stuffing in the flowers by cutting small holes in the muslin backing, and pushing in the teased-out wadding using a crochet hook (A). Use a heavy-duty or tapestry needle to thread quilting wool into the outer ring in the same way. Stitch the gaps closed.

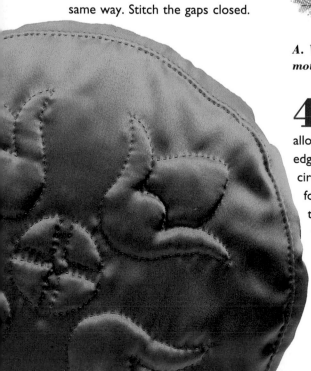

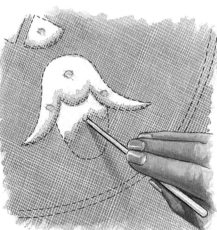

A. Work the wadding into the motif with a crochet hook.

4 Cut the circle for the front, adding 12mm / ½in seam allowances all round the outer edge. Use the template to cut a circle of paper to use as a pattern for the back of the cushion. Cut the paper pattern in half. Use the two halves to cut two pieces of cotton fabric, adding 12mm / ½in seam allowances all round.

5 Place the two halves right sides together and tack the central seam. Machine stitch 6cm / 2³⁄₈in at both ends of the seam. Place the zip right side down over the centre of the seam (B). Tack and machine stitch in place. Remove the tacking.

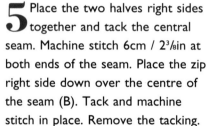
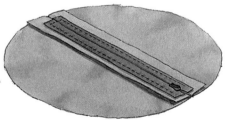

B. Place the zip on the seam and stitch it in place.

6 Place the back and front right sides together. Leaving the zip open a little to turn the cushion through, machine stitch the outside edge, snipping into the seam to ease the fabric as you go.

7 Press and turn the cushion through. Insert the pad through the open zip and close the zip.

covered HANGERS

Treat yourself and your clothing to padded coat hangers. They also make a luxury gift.

Padded coat hangers are ideal for protecting your clothes and keeping the shoulders in shape, particularly special outfits or those items of clothing that are a little delicate. Jumpers also benefit from padded coat hangers as the hanger will help the jumper to keep its shape.

If you add a herbal sachet or pomander to the padded hanger (see this chapter, Perfumed Rosebud Pomander, pp133–34), it is doubly useful, as it will help to keep the moths away.

The padding is simply strips of thin wadding which have been wrapped around a basic wooden coat hanger with the hook removed, and held in place with adhesive tape. You can then either form the fabric into a tube and feed it on to the hanger, or simply wrap the fabric around the hanger, hiding the joins with strings of beads and a bow.

Another alternative is to cut blocks of different coloured fabrics and piece them together. The resulting two-tone fabric is then sewn lengthways to make a striped tube which is gathered and fed on to the hanger. This particular method is useful for using up remnants of fabric.

Make the hangers as pretty as you can, adding ribbon bows, and give them as presents.

chapter six

making the covered hangers

When padding the hangers, don't use very thick wadding as it will make the hangers too bulky. Secure the wadding with adhesive tape – this will be hidden by the fabric.

RUCHED FLORAL COVER

1 Remove the hook from the hanger. Cut a strip of wadding 90x5cm /36x2in; secure the wadding in place with adhesive tape and wind it around the hanger. Wind some sewing thread around the wadding to secure it in place and tie in a tight knot.

A. Form even ruches of fabric along the hanger with your hand.

2 Cut the material three times longer than the hanger and 12cm / 4¾in wide. Fold in half, right sides together, and sew down the open length. Turn to the right side. Thread on to the hanger with the seam at the top. Form ruches (A), then turn in the ends and stitch them in place. Make a hole in the fabric and re-insert the hook.

3 Cut fabric 5x25cm / 2x10in long, fold it in half, right sides together, and sew along the long edge. Turn through and turn in raw edges. Gather one edge and pull up and roll the fabric so that it pleats into the base and fans out at the top to form a rose shape. Sew beneath the hook of the hanger.

STRIPY COVER

1 Remove the hook from the hanger. Cut a strip of wadding as before and secure the wadding in place with adhesive tape. Wind the wadding around the hanger then wind white thread around to secure the wadding in place. Tie the thread in a tight knot.

2 Cut six blue and five yellow pieces of fabric, each piece measuring 13x13cm / 5x5in. Sew the pieces together to form a long strip, alternating the colours as you go. Fold the strip of fabric in half lengthways and sew along the long edge. Turn to right side.

B. Run a gathering thread along the long sides of the tube and pull it in.

3 Run a gathering thread along both long edges of the strip 6mm / ¼in from the edge. Pull to gather the tube to the length of the hanger, tying the thread in a knot to secure it (B).

4 Thread the tube of ruched fabric on to the hanger. Turn in the ends and stitch in place. Ease out the gathers until they are all even, then re-insert the hook.

SILVER COVER

1 Pad the hanger with wadding as before. Cut the fabric in half across the width. With right sides facing, sew along the long sides to make two tubes. Turn right sides out. With one end against the hanger, fold the tube over itself to secure the end. Wind the tube over the hanger to the centre. Repeat with the other tube.

2 Wrap any excess fabric around the hook of the hanger and tie it in a bow. Neaten the ends with stitching if necessary.

3 Wind the beads around the hanger as with the fabric tubes (C). Following the diagonal folds, loop the beads around and under the fabric bow, then wind them round the hanger to the other end. Sew the beads in place at each end of the hanger, tucking them into a fold of fabric and securing with tiny stitches.

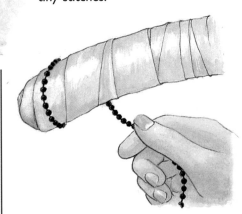

C. Wind the beads diagonally around the coat hanger.

air-drying flowers

Give fresh flowers a longer life by hanging them upside down in a cool, dry, dark place and leaving them to dry.

Air-drying is the most natural way of preserving flowers and foliage. Generally, thistles and burrs, daisy-like plants, flower heads with many tiny flowers (um-bellifers and grasses), and plants with papery bracts, calyces or seed pods are all worth trying. Strip stems as they prolong the drying time, except foliage on flowers such as cotton lavender and mimosa, which are attractive. Choose flowers that are not quite in full bloom.

Cut the flowers on a dry, warm day when there is a minimum of moisture and avoid picking when it is raining or when dew is forming. Hang the flowers in small bunches as large bunches do not allow air to circulate freely. Each bunch should contain one type of flower, as drying times vary. Some large spikes such as delphinium, mullein, bells of Ireland, bushy-headed celosias and many branched plants like burdock should be hung upside down singly. USE DRIED FLOWERS • for floral arrangements • decorating gift box-es • on hats • on wreaths, posies, pomanders • to decorate potpourri.

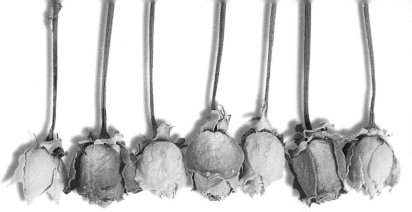

Cut the flowers before they are in full bloom. Keep the bunches small and hang them in a cool, dry place where the temperature is constant.

1 Choose only the best flowers to dry. Check that they are clean and free from dust and insects. Remove foliage from the stems (about 10cm / 4in) to prevent rotting when they are tied together.

2 Divide the flowers into small bunches, no more than four stems for each bunch. Tie them together with elastic bands or string. Check that all the foliage is removed from the stems where they make contact.

3 Wind some florist's wire around the base of the bunched stems, leaving a length of wire free to attach to the wire coathanger. Attach two or three bunches on a hanger, arranging them so they don't touch.

DRYING UPRIGHT

Some materials dry best the right way up. Chinese lanterns, for example, dry at unnatural angles if hung upside down. Simply hook one of the upper lanterns over a clothesline.

Wild grasses, some tall grasses and seed heads such as pampas, dock, bulrushes and sea lavender can be left in a dry vase.

Hydrangea, mimosa, gypsophila and delphinium dry better if stood in some water. Strip the plants of leaves as usual, then place the stems in about 5cm / 2in of water and leave in a warm room. When all the water has evaporated or been taken up by the plants, tie the stems, then hang and leave until dry.

4 Suspend the coathangers with the flowers from a shelf, rack or indoor clothesline, where they won't touch a wall. Do this in a dry room with a constant temperature and with no direct sunlight.

*Crafty*tip

Old-fashioned clothes drying racks, which can be raised and lowered, are ideal for hanging the bunches of flowers.

scented POTPOURRI

Ring the changes with a bowl of fragrant potpourri made out of a colourful arrangment of whole flower heads and petals.

Every home has its own distinctive smell and nothing adds to this more than a bowl of dried flowers you have scented and arranged yourself. Potpourri is hardly new – the ancient Egyptians and Romans used it to perfume their rooms and clothes, and the tradition is still carried on to this day.

Rose petals and lavender are generally used as a base but other flowers, such as mimosa, lilac, jasmine, lily-of-the-valley, peonies and honeysuckle, can be included. Instead of using just the petals, the potpourri here uses whole flower heads, making it attractive and original. The scent of the flowers is given added fragrance with a few drops of essential oil.

You will need

TWENTY DRIED DEEP PINK ROSES

TEN DRIED PINK PEONIES

FOUR DRIED HEADS OF PALE GREEN HYDRANGEAS

NEWSPAPER

FLORIST'S SCISSORS

10 DROPS OF ROSE OIL

BOWL OR CONTAINER

preparing the potpourri

A clear glass bowl was used here, allowing you to see the whole flower heads and the combination of colours at their best. Rose oil enhances the scent of the potpourri but you can add lavender to make your own blend.

The fragrance of the flowers fades after a while, so to freshen the arrangement, remove the whole flower heads, add a few drops of rose oil to the petals and rearrange the flower heads on top.

1 Petals on dried flowers are usually tight as they are picked while still in bud, but they can be steamed open. To do this, select the ten best roses to keep whole. Take each one by its stem so that you don't burn yourself and hold it briefly over a boiling kettle (A). Then open the petals slightly.

B. Cut the stems off just below the flower heads.

2 Separate the remaining flowers into two batches, again selecting the best ones and setting them aside to keep whole. Handle the flowers with care so that they don't break up.

3 Using the florist's scissors, cut the stems away from the flower heads (B). Do this carefully on some newspaper so that the flowers don't fall and break up.

4 Remove the petals from all the flowers that aren't being used whole (C). Again, do this carefully so that the petals don't break while you're removing them. Sprinkle with the rose oil and put them in your container.

5 Arrange the whole flower heads on top of the petals, placing the largest ones towards the centre and using the smaller ones towards to outside (D).

A. Steam the roses to open the petals out slightly.

D. Use the whole flower heads to make an attractive arrangement.

C. Pull the petals gently to break up the flower head.

perfumed rosebud POMANDER

Let the smell of summer linger all year round with this sumptuously fragrant rosebud pomander. It will perfume a room for many months to come.

Traditional fruit pomanders studded with cloves and prettily ribboned were, in the past, carried to mask odours. Nowadays, they are far more decorative and are used to add a sweet fragrance to cupboards and clothes. This elegant, scented dried-flower ball is made using a sphere of florist's foam. You can vary the types of flowers used to create different effects. They can be made very simply and the type of flowers and colours you choose will give them a touch of originality.

Masses of tiny flower heads are usually used for this kind of arrangement in order to keep the ball as round as possible. Flowers that are particularly suitable are everlasting ones, such as pearl everlasting, sandwort, strawflower, honesty, sea lavender, love-in-a-mist and masterwort. These can be bought or you could dry your own.

chapter six

arranging the pomander

To make the pomander as attractive as possible, aim for a smooth, round shape. When the fragrance fades after a while, freshen the pomander with a few drops of rose oil.

VARIATIONS

Instead of using dried rosebuds, choose other dried flowers that complement each other and decorate the pomander with coloured ribbons.

A. Push a hairpin-shaped wire through the foam.

1 Perfume the dried rosebuds with a few drops of rose oil. Make a hairpin shape by bending a stub wire in half and twisting both wires together. Push the ends of the wire through the foam ball and untwist them (A). Cut the wire, leaving 2cm / ¾ in and fold the ends back so that they are flush with the foam ball. This is to prevent the wire slipping out of the ball when it is hanging up.

2 Starting from the point where the wire was inserted, push a row of rosebud heads around the circumference of the ball. Make another circle of rosebuds so that the ball is divided into four quarters. To make it easier to hold the ball as you work, fill in first one

B. Add the rosebuds to the foam in sections.

quarter, then the quarter opposite, and so on (B). Press the rosebuds in gently, as close together as possible to cover the foam ball.

3 Slot the wide ribbon through the wire loop (C) and secure it to the wire. Tie the ribbon into a loop and let the ends trail. Wrap the ends of the narrower

ribbon around a pencil and hold the pencil over steam from a boiling kettle for a couple of minutes, to make them curl. Tie this ribbon around the wire loop for added decoration.

final touch

Check the pomander from all angles and adjust the rosebuds as necessary to make a smooth ball. Add a few drops of essential oil – rose or lavender – to finish.

C. Pull the ribbon through the wire loop and secure it in place.

You will need

17.5CM / 7IN SHORT-PILE SLEEVE
AND 17.5CM / 7IN CAGE ROLLER

10CM / 4IN HIGH-DENSITY FOAM
ROLLER AND HANDLE

HOUSEHOLD STRING

MATT EMULSION PAINT: MID BLUE,
PALE LAVENDER BLUE AND PALE
PINK ARE USED HERE

MASKING TAPE

PAINT TRAY

variations on roller painting

Interesting effects, such as stripes and random patterns, can be created using a roller tied with string.

You can create random striped effects using paint rollers, string and different coloured paints. The stripes can be as obvious or as indistinct as you like. Quite different effects are created by winding the string evenly along the foam roller, or in a random manner. You can also vary the effect by rolling the paint on horizontally, then vertically, always finishing in a vertical direction if you want to retain some illusion of stripes. Be sure to use a plumbline if you want quite definite stripes, and align the edges of the rows each time. Changing paint colour with each application in a particular direction also adds to the effect.

Choose your shades carefully – you need to use the darkest in the background then use slightly paler shades with each 'layer' or application of paint. Play around on pieces of board first before you start applying the paint to the walls – you can create wide variations in the effect depending on how you tie the string and how you layer the paint.

Finally, an interesting effect can be obtained by using the roller completely randomly over the surface, rather than trying to retain any illusion of stripes.

USE A ROLLER TIED WITH STRING • to create stripes and pattern.

Prepare the surface as necessary and apply a background colour; mid blue emulsion is used here. Tie the roller with string and do a practice run before painting a wall.

SHORT PILE ROLLER

VARIATION

Blue emulsion paint was used to cover the background surface; yellow paint was rolled on next and left to dry before applying orange paint, to give this colourful effect.

1 Take the roller sleeve, before it is attached to the roller, and secure a piece of string inside one end with masking tape. Wind the string randomly around the roller, working up to one end then back again, and securing the end inside with masking tape.

2 Fit the sleeve on to the roller, roll in the paint (pale lavender), and roll on the tray to ensure the roller surface has an even coverage of paint.

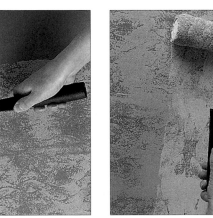

3 Apply the roller to the surface in one even sweep, working horizontal stripes first. Align or overlap the edges of the stripes. Allow to dry.

4 Prepare a new short pile roller as in Step 1 (or thoroughly wash and dry the original one). Roll in another shade of paint (pink) and roll vertical stripes in even sweeps, aligning the edges.

The first coat of paint (blue in this case) shows through the second coat (pink), giving a mottled finish.

MINI ROLLER

1 Loop the string around one end of the foam roller and knot it. Wind the string around the roller as evenly as possible, in one direction. Loop the string around the opposite end and tie securely.

2 Fit the sleeve on to the roller, roll in the first paint colour (pale lavender) and roll on the tray to give the roller an even coating of paint.

VARIATIONS
Yellow and orange applied vertically; and yellow applied horizontally and orange vertically, both on a blue background.

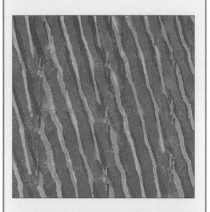

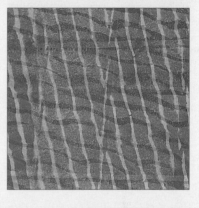

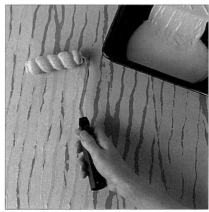

3 Apply the paint in even vertical stripes, working upwards and aligning each paint stripe with the previous one. Leave to dry.

4 Working with a new roller, or thoroughly washing and drying the first roller, apply another colour (pink) over the top, in vertical stripes, as before.

Vertical stripes using two colours.

MINI ROLLER 2

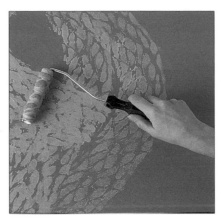

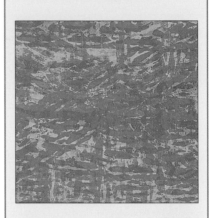

1 Tie a length of string randomly around the foam mini roller, starting at one end with a loop secured with a knot, finishing in the same way at the other end.

2 Dip the roller in the first colour of paint (pale lavender) and roll on the tray to ensure even coverage. Apply the roller randomly over the surface. Allow to dry.

VARIATIONS
Yellow and orange applied randomly; yellow applied horizontally and orange vertically, both on blue backgrounds.

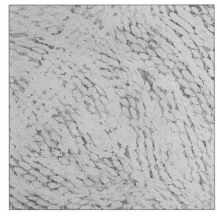

3 Prepare another foam mini roller in the same way (or wash and dry the first one thoroughly), and dip into the paint (pink), rolling it on the tray to cover it evenly. Work the roller randomly over the surface.

Two colours applied randomly creates a mottled effect.

*Crafty*tip

When painting stripes on walls, it helps to use a plumbline to keep them vertical and aligned. Start in the centre of the wall and work outwards on each side.

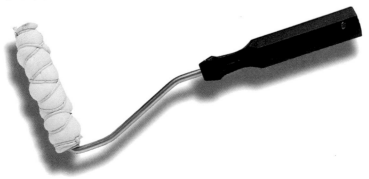

chapter seven

THE CHILDREN'S ROOM

The Children's Room

CONTENTS

simple machine-sewn
patchwork

Machine-sewing is the fastest way to assemble patchwork. Start with this easy method – it uses triangles formed into blocks to make up anything from a cushion cover to a generous quilt.

Patchwork is the traditional way to transform fabric oddments into useful, decorative items. Patches – the basic units – are assembled into shapes and then blocks (the simple method shown here joins triangles into blocks), or into rows. These in turn are sewn together into one of a galaxy of lovely designs.

Fabrics are usually plain or printed cottons, although you can use wools and velvets. They should be of similar weight and durability. Do not mix old fabrics with new.

Wash and press fabrics before you cut them. Trim the seam allowances off old fabric and check for worn patches by holding it up to the light. Line patches of fine fabric with a layer of iron-on interfacing.

USE PATCHWORK FOR • quilts • wallhangings • cushion covers.

You will need

SQUARED PATTERN PAPER

PENCIL, METAL RULER AND SET SQUARE

COLOURED PENCILS

THIN CARD

SHARP CRAFT KNIFE

FABRIC

TAILORS' CHALK OR MARKING PENCIL

SCISSORS OR ROTARY CUTTER

PINS

SEWING THREAD

SEWING MACHINE

IRON

U se this machine-sewn method to assemble triangles into blocks. Calculate the number of patches needed before buying fabric. Before you cut a template, an accurate guide to cutting shapes, decide on your finished block and use this as a guide. Sew small pieces together first, then form bigger blocks. Join patches together in the simplest way, avoiding tight corners and curved seams.

MAKING A TRIANGULAR WINDOW TEMPLATE

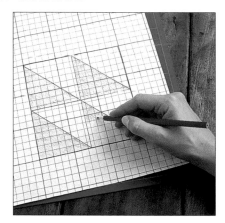

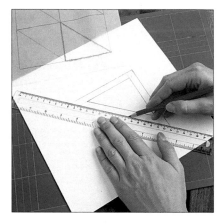

1 To make a quarter-square window template, draw up a square to the finished size of a block on a sheet of graph paper. Divide this into four squares and draw diagonals to form triangles.

2 Using coloured pencils, colour in the different sections to make up the pattern for the block. This will help you count the number of patches and calculate fabric amounts later.

3 Trace off a triangle and mark it out on thin card. Mark another line 1cm / ³⁄₈in outside the first line to allow for the seams. This is the cutting line for the fabric patches – the inner line is for stitching.

4 Using a craft knife against a metal ruler, carefully cut out along the outer edge. Then cut around the inner line in the same way. Gently push the inner triangle out to form the template.

HOW MUCH FABRIC?

For each fabric used, work out how many patches you need (including the seam allowances) then draw up a cutting plan on graph paper.

Mark the fabric width on the graph paper and work out how many patches fit across – one side of the patch must be cut with the grain. Divide the total number by the number across the width. Multiply the result by the depth of a piece when in position on the fabric. Round up to the next number to get the fabric length needed.

CUTTING OUT THE PATCHES

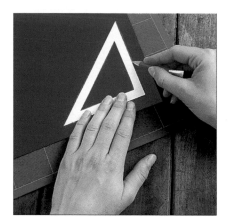

1 Position the template on the wrong side of the fabric with one edge along the straight grain. If the fabric has a distinctive pattern, mark the template on the right side, so you can choose the part of the pattern you want to use. Holding the template firmly in position, draw round the outer edge and then round the inner edge with chalk or marking pencil.

2 Mark out all the patches accurately across the fabric until you have enough for the chosen design.

*Crafty*tip

To store patches tidily, string them on to a length of thread. Either tie the thread ends together or knot at both ends.

3 Carefully cut out the triangles following the outer marked line.

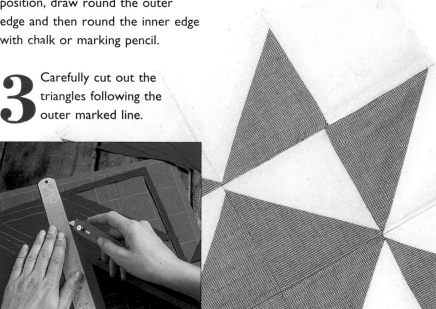

WORK BOX

A rotary cutter equipped with a retractable blade makes it easy to cut pieces neatly and accurately. Always work on a cutting mat and use a metal ruler as a guide.

JOINING PATCHES TOGETHER

  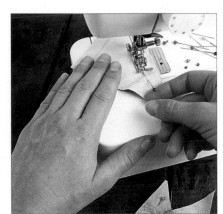

1 Lay out all the patches and decide the best way of seaming them. Sew the patches in stages, joining triangles into squares according to pattern and then into bigger blocks. For the first stage, pin together the patches, right sides facing, with the seam lines matching accurately.

2 Stitch along the seam line, removing the pins as you go. Trim the seams and press open. When joining dark and light fabrics, press the seam allowance towards the darker fabric. When pressing seams to one side, press alternate seam allowances to different sides.

3 For the second stage, seam the squares together. Pin the patches through the seam lines so they match up exactly. Sew together as before, removing the pins as you go.

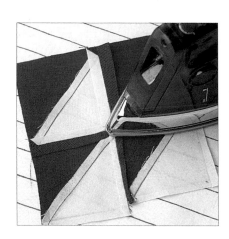

4 When the second stage is complete, press flat. To complete a block, join together along one edge, pinning across the seams as before. Stitch together as many sections as you need, then stitch these together to complete the design. Check that all the seams match, and press well.

This cushion is made up of four identical squares arranged as mirror images. Each one consists of eight triangular patches.

scent with
LOVE

Fill a small hand-sewn patchwork heart with wadding or potpourri to make an original gift. The pattern is made with hexagon templates and an assortment of remnants.

The early pioneers in America had little access to fabrics, so nothing was wasted. Larger pieces of fabric were used for quilts and any scraps were turned into gifts, often in the shape of a heart – a motif that was popular in Northern Europe, where many of the early pioneers came from. The hearts, depending on their size, were used as cushions or filled with wadding or potpourri to make gifts. Smaller sized hearts were often used as pincushions.

The hexagon, with its six sides, is an easy shape to work and lends itself well to a random design. It is also used for formal patchwork designs.

making the hearts

The two main patchwork units are made by hand. They are then trimmed into a heart shape and joined back to back. The heart is finally filled with lavender, potpourri or cushion wadding.

Enlarge templates to twice this size (see Enlarging a Design, p6).

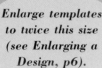

1 Enlarge and trace the hexagon on to card using carbon paper and cut it out with a craft knife. Place template on glossy paper and cut 20 templates. Pin templates on to fabrics, matching one straight edge with the straight grain of the fabric. Cut out with a 1cm / ³⁄₈in seam allowance.

2 Fold seam allowance over paper templates and tack, folding each corner. Make 20 patches. Place two patches, with right sides together, and oversew two straight edges together, spacing 16-18 stitches to 2.5cm / 1in and securing with an extra stitch at the start and finish of each edge. Keeping the needle threaded, open the patches out.

A. Draw around the template to make a heart shape.

B. Attach insertion piping.

3 Select another patch and place it, right sides together, over the first patch and repeat the oversewing. Try to select patches so that each side of the hexagon is beside a hexagon of a different colour or pattern.

C. Stitch along sewn line.

4 Join more patches to make a top row of four, a second row of three, a third row of two and a final single patch. Make a second unit of 10 patches, varying the pattern from the first patch. Remove all the paper templates. Press the units with seam allowances on to the relevant patch.

5 Enlarge, trace and cut out the heart motif to make a paper template. Place it on the wrong side of a unit so the point rests in the middle of the single patch and the top notch lies at the top in the middle of the unit. Pin in place and draw round the template with french chalk or a water-soluble pen (A).

D. Trim excess fabric and snip the curves.

6 Pin insertion piping so stitching lies along drawn line and overlaps on a long side of the heart. Stitch piping to work, along stitched line on piping (B). If machining, use a zip foot.

7 Place the second unit face down on to the first unit, matching the patches, and pin in place. Stitch together from the wrong side of the first unit, stitching along the row of stitching holding the piping (C). Leave a 7.5cm / 3in gap along one side. Trim away surplus fabric and clip curves and points (D). Turn unit through to right side; press. Fill with wadding, lavender or potpourri (E). Stitch the gap together to finish.

E. Fill the heart with stuffing.

four-seasons PATCHWORK

Four patchwork house blocks, one for each season, are used to make a wall hanging.

The hand-quilted houses reflect the bright colours of spring, vivid summer, russet autumn and a white winter. Look for appropriate fabrics – red for roofs, except for winter when white would be better. Choose different floral fabrics to make the garden for each season.

You will need to make two house block templates (one to cut up), with the patches carefully measured. Use graph paper to copy the design, and outline the shapes you need in four horizontal rows. Number each patch, and make a note of which fabric you need for which patch. When you cut out your material, remember to leave a seam allowance of 6mm / ¼in.

making the wall hanging

Each house block is made up in units that make four horizontal rows, which are then joined to complete the house. The finished size of the patchwork wall hanging is 75x75cm / 30x30in square.

FABRIC REQUIREMENTS

A SELECTION OF FABRICS TO SUGGEST THE FOUR SEASONS FOR THE SKY, ROOFS, GARDENS, DOORS AND WINDOWS

46CM / 18IN FABRIC 114CM / 45IN WIDE, FOR THE HOUSES

10CM / 4IN FABRIC 114CM / 45IN WIDE, FOR THE HOUSE DETAILS

120CM / 48IN FABRIC 114CM / 45IN WIDE FOR THE SASHING, BORDERS AND BACKING

90CM / 36IN WADDING

1 Select and press all the fabrics, and group into seasons. Cut paper templates and use them to cut all the fabric pieces, using a quilter's ruler and rotary cutter. Sort all the pieces into seasons,

2 Hand-sew small pieces together to make four units of four horizontal rows. Machine the units to make the house block.

3 Trim blocks to 31.5cm / 12½in square. Cut two joining strips 6.5x31.5cm / 2½x12½in and sew these below the spring and summer blocks, right sides together, taking 1cm / ⅜in seams. Press, then attach the strips to the tops of the autumn and winter blocks, right sides together, taking 1cm / ⅜in seams.

4 Cut three strips 6.5x66.5cm / 2½x26½in and sew these between and on each side of the two previously joined blocks, right sides together, with 1cm / ⅜in seams. Press the blocks.

5 Cut two strips 6.5x76cm / 2½x30½in. Sew right sides together to the top and bottom, taking 1cm / ⅜in seams.

6 Place the wall hanging over a piece of wadding cut to the same size and place both these pieces on top of the backing fabric placed wrong side up.

7 Grid tack, then quilt around each block and around the houses, doors and windows.

8 Cut a strip of backing fabric 74x11cm / 29x4¼in to make a hanging sleeve. Turn in a 1cm / ⅜in hem down either short side and machine stitch. Place on top of the wall hanging at the back, centred, with wrong side of strip to right side of backing, aligning the raw edges at the top. Tack in place. Fold in 1cm / ⅜in at the base of the sleeve and catch-stitch to the back of the wall hanging. (A).

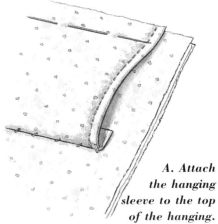

A. Attach the hanging sleeve to the top of the hanging.

9 Cut strips of fabric on the bias and bind the outside edge, taking in the top of the sleeve.

10 Hang, using a wooden pole or brass rod in the sleeve. To make a feature of it, make sure the pole protrudes at each end. Otherwise, hide the ends behind the wall hanging.

using
felt

A novel way of creating appliqué motifs is to use brightly coloured felt, which is easy to apply.

Felt is a wonderful material to work with as it does not fray, comes in bright clear colours and is particularly suited to children's projects. A washable craft felt is now available in handy narrow widths.

The simple appliqué technique shown here features fish, which are easy to draw and come in many shapes and tropical colours, giving you the opportunity to be as creative as you like. The checked fabric gives a folk feeling to the work. Shapes can be cut out direct, but rather than trying to draw on the felt, first work out your design on paper, cut it out and use this as a pattern for the appliqué.

To add interest, pinking shears, as well as straight scissors are used here to cut out the motifs, which are stitched with a small running stitch as well as blanket stitch.

USE FELT APPLIQUE • to decorate children's clothing • to decorate holdalls • to make wall hangings.

You will need

PIECE OF CHECK BASE FABRIC 25x37CM / 10x14½IN

PIECES OF FELT

IRON

PENCIL AND PAPER

PINS

BUTTONHOLE THREAD

PINKING SHEARS

SCISSORS

SEWING NEEDLE

Felt doesn't fray, and is easy to sew. Use
different types of decorative stitching to add
extra interest.

1 Press all the fabrics. Draw some fishes, about 15x9cm / 6x3½in on a piece of paper and cut them out.

2 Select the colours and pin the fish patterns to the appropriate coloured felt and cut out.

3 Pin the motifs to the backing fabric. Choose a contrasting or matching thread and sew the fishes on, using running stitch worked close to the edge.

4 Cut some small circles from tiny squares of contrasting felt and, using pinking shears, cut out wave shapes and stripes for the fish. Add these to the design.

5 Attach the pieces to the fishes by sewing a cross-stitch in the centre of each circle, passing the thread at the back of the checked fabric. Add felt eyes and mouths to the fishes.

You will need

COTTON DRILL

GESSO PRIMER

SCISSORS

VINYL SILK EMULSION PAINT

PENCIL AND PAPER

CUTOUTS FOR DECOUPAGE

GLOSS MEDIUM VARNISH

MATT VARNISH

découpaged cotton drill

Paper cutouts on cotton is an unusual combination, but the end result is very effective if you choose the right colours and cutouts.

Hard-wearing and easy to clean, these cloth mats can be created using a wide variety of paper patterns on coated cotton drill. The basic mat is cut from cotton drill, given two coats of gesso and then cut to size so that it won't fray. Two or three coats of paint are then applied to the mat and when this is dry, the chosen cutouts are set in place, using varnish to secure them. The finished mat is sealed with varnish, to protect the design and to give an element of heat resistance.

You can choose a variety of images for the découpage. Use photocopies taken from books and magazines, images from wrapping paper and patterns from wallpaper to complement the room decor.

The same method can be used to create a floor cloth, ideal for the nursery, bedroom or dining room. If the surface shows signs of wear it can be retouched with varnish.

USE DECOUPAGED COTTON • for table mats • floor cloths.

151

The mats shown measure 38x28cm / 15x11in and are cut from cotton drill available from fabric shops and yacht chandlers. The gesso primer is available from arts and crafts shops and decorator's suppliers.

A tester pot of emulsion paint should be enough to complete the mats.

1 Cut a rectangle of cotton drill slightly larger than the size required. Apply two coats of gesso on one side of the cloth – it doesn't matter which side of the cotton you use.

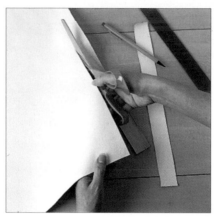

2 When dry, use a pencil and ruler to mark out and cut a rectangle just within the outer edge, to give you a clean, firm line for the finished cloth. Use scissors to do the cutting.

3 Apply two or three coats of emulsion paint to the cloth, allowing each coat to dry completely before applying the next coat of paint.

4 Use cuticle scissors to cut out the découpage images and apply them to the cloth using gloss medium varnish. Smooth the cutouts down well.

VARIATIONS

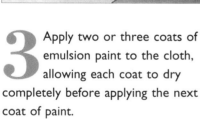

An olive green background complements the colours of the découpaged images.

The intricate detail of the cutouts gives the découpage a three-dimensional quality.

5 When dry, give the cloth two coats of gloss medium varnish and three coats of matt varnish, allowing each coat to dry before applying the next.

no-sew
BLINDS

Quick to make, these blinds give your windows a pretty, country touch or a cheerful seaside look. All they require is careful planning and measuring.

You will need

IRON AND BOARD

PRESSING CLOTH

FABRIC
(SEE MEASURING, BELOW)

TAPE MEASURE

SCISSORS

BUMPER PACK OF SELF-ADHESIVE
HEMMING TAPE

FABRIC GLUE

PINS

TIES: 5MM ROPE OR 5CM / 2IN
WIDE SOFT-FURNISHING RIBBON
OR BRAID, 4 X LENGTH OF FABRIC

STICK'N'STICK VELCRO,
2 X THE WIDTH OF THE
COMPLETE BLIND

8 SEA URCHIN SHELLS WITH HOLES

Making these no-sew blinds couldn't be simpler. They are fixed (so they cannot be used on windows that need more than a decorative effect), you'll run them up without a stitch and they can give a room a completely new look.

A firm-weave cotton or chintz is ideal as material and a lightweight fabric, such as lace, can also be used for a pretty, frothy effect. A floral chintz looks ravishing trimmed with a coordinating ribbon. A blue and white striped fabric, trimmed with rope and shells, is perfect for a seaside look. Avoid heavy velvets or linen union, as they are too bulky.

MEASURING

The width of the fabric must be at least 2.5-5cm / 1-2in wider than the window to make a firm turned-under edge. The length required is that of the window plus 15-18cm / 6-7in for the top and bottom (the bottom is turned over twice).

The length of ribbon or rope required is four times the length of the window. Trim the ties once the blinds are in position so there isn't too much tie left dangling.

153

making the blinds

Although the ties differ, the two blinds are made in the same way. The floral print is tied with ribbons and the striped blind uses rope decorated with shells.

1 To make the floral-print blind, press the fabric on the wrong side and cut to size. Turn the selvedge sides over and secure with hemming tape, as per pack instructions. Turn the bottom hem under twice. Use fabric glue, following the manufacturer's instructions, for the second fold, and press. Turn over 5cm / 2in on the top edge, using hemming tape.

2 Place the blind right side down. Divide the top width into three equal sections and mark them with pins. Cut the ribbon in half. Fold each length into two and mark the fold with a pin. Position a ribbon along the blind so that the pin aligns with the pin at the top edge of the blind. Glue 5cm / 2in of ribbon to the top edge of the fabric and press. Repeat with the other ribbon and leave to dry. Remove pins.

3 Place the blind wrong side down and fold the ribbons over the blind so that they align with the ribbons on the other side. Glue 5cm / 2in of the ribbon to the top edge of the fabric as before. Repeat with the second ribbon and leave to dry.

STRIPED BLIND

Divide the width into four sections (see Step 2). Ignore the centre and and mark the outer two sections with pins. Glue the rope to the top edge on both sides of the blind. Hang the blind and then attach the shells. Thread a shell, with the small hole at the top, and knot the rope below. Pull the knot into the shell. Repeat with the other shells.

A. Attaching the Velcro

4 Place the blind right side down. Cut two strips of Velcro the same length as the width of the blind. Stick a strip of Velcro along the top edge (A). Stick the second piece of Velcro down alongside and butting up against the first.

5 Stick two corresponding pieces of Velcro on to the flat area of the window where the blind is to be fixed or on to a wooden batten screwed in position, if this is more suitable.

6 Attach the back of the blind to the Velcro against the window. Arrange the fabric into neat folds, so that it concertinas up to the required height in the centre, with the outside sections draping down. Tie the ribbons into bows and trim the ends diagonally.

stencilled
CHEST OF DRAWERS

A stencil is used to create the woolly body of the sheep and details, such as the legs, are added freehand using a permanent marker.

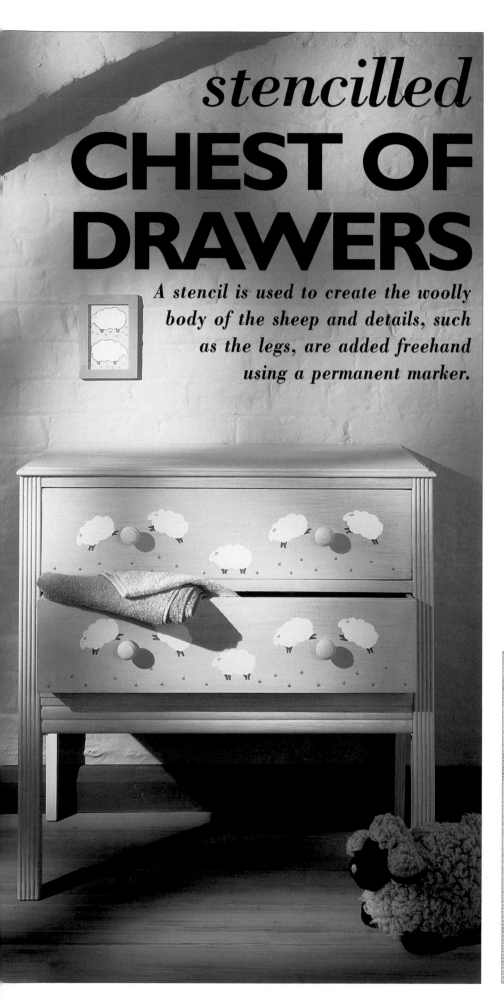

A number of wonderfully fluffy sheep are stencilled on to a bedroom chest of drawers to look as if they are jumping over the drawer handles every now and again, giving a new interpretation to the traditional counting of sheep by the sleepless.

The chest is brushed over with matt vinyl emulsion paint in a selection of pastel shades lightly blended together. White emulsion is used to stencil the sheep and their legs are drawn on with a grey permanent marker, being careful to capture the correct angle of movement. Tiny tufts of grass are created with a stencil crayon, which helps to give fine definition. A fine black marker is used for the eyes, ears and noses.

The stencil would also be very effective worked as a border around the walls of a room, either at ceiling height or dado-rail level. In this case, work several marching sheep, interspersed with a couple of leaping sheep. If you apply the emulsion paint quite thickly when stencilling the sheep, it will give the appearance of a woolly coat.

You will need

CHEST OF DRAWERS
MEDIUM-GRADE SANDPAPER
CLOTH
MATT VINYL EMULSION IN PALE PINK, PALE LILAC, PALE LIME GREEN AND WHITE
PAINTBRUSHES
SPRAY-ON ADHESIVE
STENCIL
STENCIL BRUSH
DARK GREY AND BLACK FINE-TIPPED PERMANENT MARKER
GREEN STENCIL CRAYON
SCRAP PAPER
CLEAR ACRYLIC VARNISH, OPTIONAL

stencilling the sheep

Prepare the chest by sanding it down, as necessary, to prime the surface, and wipe it to remove any dust.

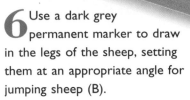

1 Paint the chest in a patchy fashion with pale pink and pale lilac emulsion using a fairly dry brush. Leave to dry.

2 Using a clean dry brush, apply a little pale lime green over the surface to blend the other colours without obscuring them (A).

B. Add the legs to the stencilled sheep using a permanent marker.

A. Apply the lime paint with a dry brush and blend the colours lightly.

3 Use spray-on adhesive to set the stencil towards the lower edge in the centre of each drawer. Using a stencil brush, stipple on white emulsion.

4 Cutting down the stencil if necessary so it fits around the drawer handles, stencil sheep at an angle around each handle, so the sheep appear to be jumping. Leave the stencils to dry.

5 Reposition the stencil and stipple the sheep again to create a woolly appearance. Use the paint quite thickly so it appears textured for the best effect. Leave to dry.

6 Use a dark grey permanent marker to draw in the legs of the sheep, setting them at an appropriate angle for jumping sheep (B).

7 Work some green stencil crayon on to some paper and use a stencil brush to apply green grass tufts along the base of the stencilled design.

8 Stencil two rows of standing sheep on the sides of the chest, in line with the drawers. Add legs and grass tufts, as before.

9 Use a black permanent marker to draw in the eyes, ears and noses on the stencils (C).

C. Draw the eyes, ears and noses using a permanent marker.

final touch

If the chest is to be used in a child's or baby's room, you can seal the surface of the chest with one or two coats of clear acrylic varnish.

paper pulp PICTURE

The picture is built up with coloured paper pulp textured with a variety of items. The pulp is shaped on a frame to create the landscape and left to dry before being framed.

The appeal of this picture is its naive quality which has all the simplicity of a child's drawing. It's inexpensive to make as it is consists mainly of scrap paper. Collect bits of paper so that you have a good supply for making the pulp. Use soft paper such as tissue. Avoid newspaper for this project. The texture is created by adding anything from threads to dried flower leaves and you can experiment with anything else you have to hand.

You can use the same method to make greetings cards. For example, for a birthday, you can build up a motif on the frame to include the age of the recipient or create an image to reflect their favourite pastime or hobby. Although the pulp is coloured before making the picture, you can keep it plain and use water-based ink or paints to colour the dry pulp and to add any other details.

making the paper picture

Take equal parts tissue paper and water. Soak the paper in the water for several hours. Pulp the mixture in an electric liquidizer. If the pulp is too dense, add water.

1 Make the basic pulp, as described above.

2 Copy and enlarge the picture above to measure 25x25cm / 10x10in on to a piece of blank paper for reference, noting the relevant colours and where you are going to use them.

3 Divide the pulp into six small containers and colour them yellow, blue, green, red, dark green and crimson. Don't add too much colour as more can be painted on later if necessary.

A. Use the coloured pulp on the frame to create the picture.

4 Choose a different texture for each coloured pulp and stir to mix these in thoroughly. In the picture shown, cloves were added to the red pulp, tarragon leaves to the light green pulp, beads to the dark green pulp, potpourri to the crimson pulp and coloured cotton to the blue pulp. The yellow pulp was left plain.

5 Place the frame mesh side up on a flat surface covered with towels. Build the picture up on the mesh, segment by segment, pinching the pulp into shape with your fingertips and following your reference diagram. Working from one end of the frame, make the pulp shapes quite thick (A). Graduate the thickness of the other shapes to gain a feeling of perspective.

B. With the pulp in position, use a modelling tool to add detail.

6 Use a modelling tool or the end of a paintbrush to shape and mould the pulp and to round off any corners or edges (B).

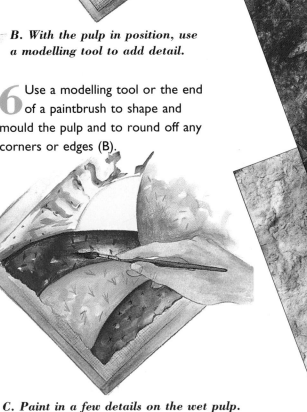

C. Paint in a few details on the wet pulp.

7 While the pulp is still wet, use the water-based inks or paints to add some detail and to highlight some areas (C) so that the colours in the final picture won't appear flat. When the pulp is completely dry, remove it from the frame and display it as desired.

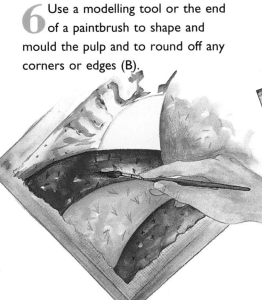

paper WINDMILLS

*Use the windmills to decorate your child's room.
Set them where a draught keeps them turning.*

These windmills make great decorations and they work too. Colour theme them for a tasteful alternative to dried flowers and set a bunch of them in a vase, or use hologram paper, available from craft shops and graphic suppliers, for a really glitzy special effect.

They are simple to make from coloured squares of stiff paper, following a technique probably half-remembered from childhood.

Cut towards the centre of a square of paper to create the sails of the windmill. Glue in place, then attach the windmill to a length of dowelling using a moulding pin, allowing the head to protrude far enough for the windmill to revolve. Blow the windmills or place them in a breeze and they will spin.

For a child's outdoor party, set them in small pots filled with sand, but avoid leaving them out in strong winds.

You will need

PENCIL

RULER

15x15CM / 6x6IN SQUARES OF
STIFF COLOURED PAPER

SCISSORS

PAPER GLUE

EMULSION PAINT IN A COLOUR TO
TONE WITH THE PAPER

PAINTBRUSH

EMPTY BOTTLE OR JAM JAR

ONE 36CM / 14IN LENGTH OF
12MM / ½IN DOWELLNG FOR EACH
WINDMILL

15MM / ⅝IN MOULDING PINS

HAMMER

making the paper windmills

Use fairly stiff paper to make the windmills. Choose complementary or contrasting colours, according to the final effect you wish to create. Papers with a metallic finish work well. Avoid heavily textured handmade papers.

Craftytip

Instead of cutting a straight edge when doing the diagonals on the squares, use pinking shears to create a more interesting edge.

ALTERNATIVE DESIGN

When using hologram paper, which is backed with white, colour this with a felt-tip pen so that the shiny paper picks up the colour. Secure the corners with a moulding pin without using glue.

A. Turn the corner of the paper in towards the centre of the square and secure it with a dab of glue.

1 Using a pencil and ruler, draw two lines diagonally from corner to corner across the squares of paper.

2 Cut 8.5cm / 3¼in in along the lines from each corner. Fold the corners gently into the centre and secure with a dab of glue (A). If varying the sizes to make smaller and larger windmills, cut each diagonal to within about 12mm / ½in of the centre, where the two diagonal lines cross.

3 Paint the dowelling, including the ends, and allow to dry. To make this easier, paint half the length of the dowelling and stand it in an empty bottle to dry, then paint the remaining section and leave to dry.

4 Cut a paper circle 12mm / ½in in diameter and place it in the centre of the windmill. Hammer a moulding pin through the centre into the dowelling about 3cm / 1¼in down from one end, allowing the head to protrude about 6mm / ¼in from the dowelling.

stencilling with crayons

Specially made stencil crayons allow you to add background colour and a motif to a surface.

If you have never stencilled before and are daunted at the thought of using paint, try crayons to get the basic feel of the technique. Crayons allow you to play around with no fear of mess – they are dry, so there is no risk of colour bleeding under the stencil.

Strictly speaking they're not crayons but handy sticks of oil-based paint that are used with a stencilling brush to create quick patterns on a variety of surfaces. The crayons can be found at arts and crafts shops, and some DIY stores. They are available in several colours – the primaries, white and a few other subtler shade variations. The crayons are relatively expensive, but last for a long time. If you invest in three primary colours, you can mix most other colours. Because the paint is in a stick form and is wrapped in paper, it is easy to handle and you have good control of the colour.

Even though the texture of the crayons is quite dry, you must allow each area to dry thoroughly before you move on to the next section.

USE STENCILLING CRAYONS ON • walls • frames • wood surfaces • painted or papered walls.

MIXING COLOURS

You can combine crayons to mix more colours in two ways:

1 Rub the first colour on to card and place the second colour on top. Mix the colours with the stencil brush to create the new colour.

2 Place the first colour on card and use the brush to apply it to the chosen surface. Place the second colour on card and brush it on to the first to blend it.

Rub the crayons on a piece of paper to remove any surface finish before you start. Don't use the crayon directly on a surface as the paint has a thick, sticky texture that must be applied with a brush. Practise using the crayons on a piece

1 Rub the crayon in a circle on a piece of spare card. Rub the stencil brush in the colour in a circular motion.

2 Fill in the background colour, applying the stencil brush in a random manner over the surface.

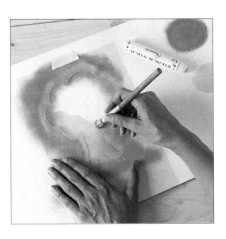

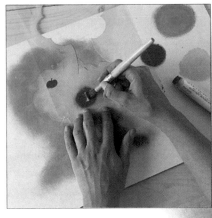

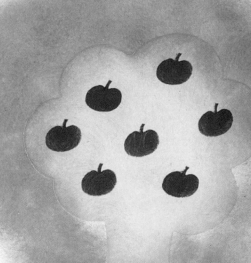

3 Secure the stencil in place with masking tape and take up more crayon colour on the brush. Stipple in the cutout areas and leave to dry.

4 Apply another colour as before and leave to dry. If doing more than one motif, apply all of one colour, moving the stencil as necessary.

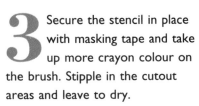

final touch

Highlights can be added to the motif by using a white crayon. Take up colour on the brush and lightly shade the motif as required.

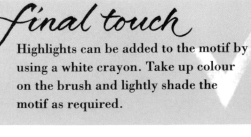

You will need
SCRUBBED POTATO
SMALL, SHARP KNIFE
FELT-TIP PEN
KITCHEN ROLL
EMULSION OR ACRYLIC PAINT
FLAT BRUSH
CLEAR POLYURETHANE VARNISH,
OPTIONAL

potato printing

Potato printing, a memory of childhood days, is actually an excellent method of printing on a variety of surfaces such as wood and paper, and can also be used to add colour and pattern to painted surfaces.

To make effective potato prints, use a sharp knife to cut your design. Cut the potato in half to give you a flat surface. Then cut another sliver from the cut side to make sure it is completely flat.

The size of the print is limited by the size of the potato. If you want to make quite a big print, choose a large baking potato and cut it along its length rather than its width, to provide the largest possible surface for the motif to be printed.

Mark the design for the print on the flat cut side using a felt-tip pen if you need a guideline. Cut the unwanted part of the potato away with the knife to leave you with neat edges then apply paint to the surface using a small brush. This is more controllable than dipping the cut potato directly into the paint and then printing it. You will get about four prints of varying strengths from the potato before you need to brush on more paint.

You can also get a two-tone effect by brushing paint in toning colours on to each half of the design.

USE POTATO PRINTS • on walls • on wooden items • to decorate previously painted surfaces.

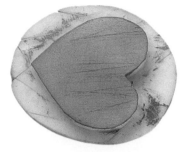
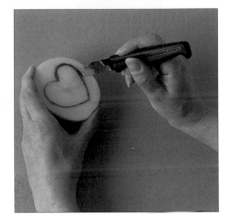

Use a small sharp knife with a straight rather than serrated edge to cut the motif in the potato.

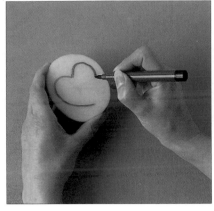

1 Cut the potato in half then shave off a fine sliver to provide a completely flat surface. Pat the cut surface dry with kitchen paper.

2 Using a felt-tip pen, draw the outline of the motif on the cut surface. Don't make the motif too intricate or complex and allow a small margin on the outside.

3 Holding the knife upright, cut down vertically into the potato and following the outline of the motif to a depth of about 12mm / ½ in.

STOP
If the print has an uneven surface, rub the cut surface of the potato up and down on a piece of smooth wood, then print again.

5 Brush paint on to the motif, being careful not to apply too much. Print the motif. Make three or four prints and then reload the potato with paint.

4 Cut horizontally across the potato to meet the vertical cuts. Ease the unwanted part of the potato away, leaving a stamp effect.

final touch

Leave the paint to dry then seal with clear polyurethane varnish if required.

THE BATHROOM

The Bathroom

CONTENTS

trompe l'oeil effects

Use this technique to add another dimension to a room by changing its proportions – the final effect is a decorative illusion.

Trompe l'oeil, meaning literally 'to deceive the eye', consists of painting an image on a flat surface to give a three-dimensional effect, for example, a displaycase painted on a wall, or a scene created to extend a feature within the room.

Trompe l'oeil is usually painted freehand, but for the sake of the beginner, a geometric design is used here to help to get to grips with the principles. An understanding of how light and shade create form is essential, because you need to reproduce that effect. When creating highlights and shadows, don't go for the stark contrast of black and white. Instead, mix a little white or black into your base colour and use very dark and very light shades of this colour to give form.

USE TROMPE L'OEIL • to add interest to a room • to extend a feature • to change the perspective.

You will need

EMULSION PAINT FOR THE BACKGROUND COLOUR

PAINTBRUSH OR ROLLER

PENCIL

RULER

PAIR OF COMPASSES OR A PAPER CUP

WHITE CHINAGRAPH

BLACK AND WHITE ARTIST'S ACRYLIC PAINT

FLAT ARTIST'S PAINTBRUSH

ERASER

FINE ARTIST'S PAINTBRUSH

The technique is used here to create a door on a wall panel. Paint the wall or panel with emulsion paint in the colour of your choice (blue is used here).

HOW LIGHT AND SHADE CREATE FORM

Successful trompe l'oeil depends on an understanding of form and how light and shade affects it to give a three-dimensional effect. The effect of light and shade on an object depends on the direction of the light source. So when planning a trompe l'oeil, you need to check the area being painted and shade it accordingly. For example, if the light (or window) is to the left of the surface being painted, the shadows will fall to the right. If you reverse this, the end result won't look natural.

Look at the black and white pictures. In the one on the left, the light is coming from the right so the right-hand areas of the objects are highlighted, while the other side is in the shade. The reverse is true in the picture on the right. The variations in tone, that is the shading from white to grey, give form to the objects, whatever their shape and regardless of the source of the directional light.

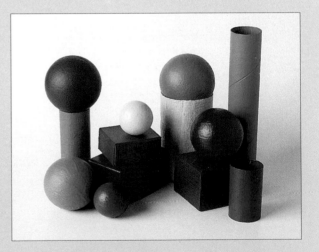

Colour takes the exercise in black and white a step further, and once you understand the effect of light and shade on a white object you can use this knowledge to create form on a coloured object. The highlight and shade are less obvious, but you will see how the form of each object is created by a colour variation from light to dark. You will need to observe this when mixing your paints to create a trompe l'oeil effect – subtle gradations of tone are essential to create a realistic shape which appears to be three dimensional.

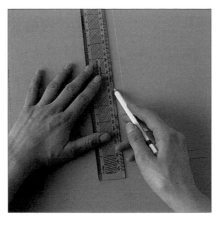

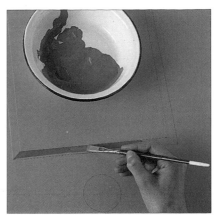

1 Draw two panels using a pencil and ruler to resemble those of a door. Draw parallel lines about 1cm / ⅔ in away. Draw evenly spaced circles down one edge using a pair of compasses, or draw around a paper cup. Draw diagonal lines across the panel corners to mitre the edges.

2 Use a white chinagraph to go over the pencil outlines on the sides of the panels to be the highlights, that is the direction from which the light is coming. These will be in the same position on each panel – if these aren't consistent, the effect of light and shade won't work.

3 Mix some black paint into the background colour to create a shade of grey dark enough to give the illusion of depth and shadow. Paint in the sides of the panels opposite to the white areas, using a flat artist's paintbrush. Leave to dry.

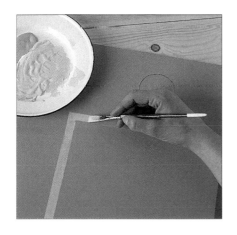

4 Mix white into the background colour and paint in the outlined sections of the panel, observing the mitred corners where the white joins the grey.

5 Use the white chinagraph again to outline the outer edge of the highlighted area of the panels to neaten the line and to give it a straight edge.

6 Use an eraser to soften the line and blend it in to the area painted in the lighter shade, not the background colour.

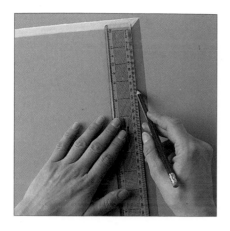

7 With a ruler and pencil, draw along the inner edge of the grey shadow area on the panels to give a sharp edge.

8 Using a fine artist's brush, paint shadow on half of the circles, which represent studs in the door, corresponding to shaded areas on the panels. Taper the shadow at each end.

9 Mix a paler grey paint and highlight the other side of the circles, using a fine artist's paintbrush and tapering the ends to overlap with the darker curve of the circles.

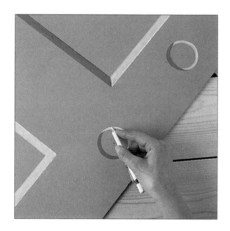

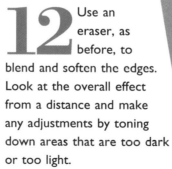

10 Use a white chinagraph in the same way as before around the outer edge of the highlighted areas to give a crisper outline to the shapes.

11 Use a pencil freehand around the inner edge of the shaded area to add emphasis.

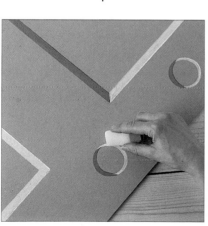

12 Use an eraser, as before, to blend and soften the edges. Look at the overall effect from a distance and make any adjustments by toning down areas that are too dark or too light.

shower CURTAIN

Add an original touch to your bathroom with a shower curtain you have made and decorated yourself.

Making your own shower curtain is a wonderful way of ensuring that your curtain is not only individual, but that it matches the decor of your bathroom, as it can be hard to find a curtain that is just the right colour or pattern to suit.

By setting images of your choice on the curtain beneath a layer of clear self-adhesive plastic, you can create your own personal design. Silhouettes cut from black paper, fabric cutouts taken from that used for blinds or curtains, images from magazines with their backs lined with paper and tinted photocopies are all suitable and can be chosen with a particular theme in mind.

Make sure that the images are applied to the outside of the shower curtain and then covered with clear plastic to prevent water damage. Buy the clear PVC for the curtain in a roll – do not allow it to be folded as it will be hard to eradicate the creases.

Hang the shower curtain from an existing rail using metal eyelets. These are available in a kit, complete with fixing tools plus plastic hooks. You can adjust the length of the curtain to suit simply by trimming the bottom. To clean the curtain, wipe it down regularly with a sponge on the inside, avoiding the outer surface.

You will need

CLEAR GLASS PVC, ABOUT 200x130CM / 79x51IN (THE DROP WILL DEPEND ON THE HEIGHT OF THE SHOWER RAIL)

SCISSORS

IRON

MASKING TAPE

STICKY-BACKED PLASTIC

TAPE MEASURE

EYELET KIT

SHINY PAPER IN LEMON, LIME AND ORANGE

SPRAY-ON ADHESIVE

CRAFT KNIFE

HOLE PUNCH

chapter eight

making the curtain

Work on a flat dust-free surface as PVC has a tendency to create static and pick up dust.

1 Turn the top end of the PVC over by about 2.5cm / 1in, using masking tape to hold it at intervals.

2 Place a strip of coated paper (use the backing paper from the clear adhesive film used in Step 8), glossy side down over the hem edge and press it with a hot iron, being careful not to touch the iron to the PVC.

3 Turn the top hem over again and press again using the coated paper and a hot iron, to bond the plastic to itself (A).

B. Cover the motifs with sticky-backed plastic.

lemon, lime and orange. Cut out smaller circles of white card and use the template, right, to cut out wagon-wheel shapes. Apply the shapes to the circles using spray-on adhesive. Cut the finished pieces in half to create fruit halves.

7 Arrange the fruit on one side of the curtain. Use a hole punch to punch out small circles of coloured paper to represent bubbles to add to the design.

8 Apply spray-on adhesive to the back of the fruit and attach lightly to the curtain. Cut pieces of clear self-adhesive plastic to fit over the whole design, allowing 12mm / ½in extra margin all round (B).

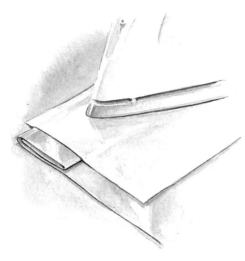

A. Bond the plastic by ironing it.

4 Measure across the top edge and mark the positions for the eyelets, spacing them evenly, with the end ones quite close together.

5 Following instructions on the packet, attach the eyelets to the top edge through all thicknesses of the PVC.

6 Cut circles of paper in the required colours, for example

9 Cut circles of sticky-backed plastic twice the diameter of the paper ones to coat the bubbles on the curtain. Set the bubbles in place and cover with sticky-backed plastic.

10 Hang the curtain so that the smooth side of the PVC faces in towards the shower and the applied patterns are on the outside.

The lining for the blind is attached in such a way that it forms a border on the front. To show it at its best, choose your fabric accordingly, using complementary or contrasting colours, striped or patterned.

The blind has a self-lining made in the same striped fabric which is also used to create a border on the sides and lower edge on the front of the blind. The front of the blind is cut with horizontal stripes and the back or lining is cut larger with vertical stripes which also form the borders. It can equally well be made using a plain fabric or a printed floral fabric with a toning colour for the self-lining.

Roman blinds are ideal in the bathroom, where conventional curtains may look fussy and take up valuable space.

You will need

120CM / 47¼IN WIDE STRIPED FABRIC; FOR LENGTH, SEE OVERLEAF

MATCHING THREAD

4M / 13½FT ROMAN BLIND TAPE

SCISSORS

TAPE MEASURE

STICK-AND-SEW FASTENER, SUCH AS VELCRO

SEWING MACHINE

LATH, THE WIDTH OF THE BLIND

BATTEN, THE WIDTH OF THE WINDOW

lined roman BLIND

Back panel

Front panel

A. The front and back are joined to make a tube, which is then turned right side out.

making the blind

To create horizontal stripes, the front panel of the blind is made using the width of the fabric for the depth. If the drop required is more than the width of the fabric, increase the length of the back panel to compensate. For the front panel, measure the depth of the window less 5cm / 2in plus 3mm / ^{1}/$_8$in for each fold in the blind; the width is that of the window less 20cm / 8in plus seam allowances. For the back panel width, add on 20cm / 8in for the borders plus seam allowances; for the depth, add on 10cm / 4in for the border at the bottom, allow 5cm / 2in for the top and bottom hems plus 3mm / ^{1}/$_8$in for each fold.

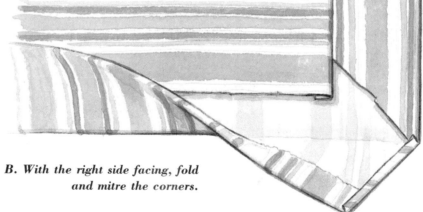

B. With the right side facing, fold and mitre the corners.

1 With the right sides together, and aligning the top edges, join the front and back of the fabric to make a tube. Press the seam allowances away from the front centrepiece. Turn the tube through and press to form an even border at each side (A).

2 Press 2.5cm / 1in at the base of the lining to the wrong side. Slipstitch to the front panel along the fold, turning in and trimming the corners at the front to create a mitred effect (B). Press and tack the corners.

3 Sew across the top of the fabric through both thicknesses to help keep the layers together while you work.

4 Attach the roman blind tape to the fabric and sew across the blind to form folds at regular intervals.

5 Sew a strip of fastener to the top of the blind, pressing 2.5cm / 1in to the wrong side first.

6 Glue or staple a corresponding strip to the piece of wood to be used as a batten at the top of the window. Paint the wood first to match your colour scheme, or cover it with a piece of spare fabric, gluing it in place before attaching the batten to the wall.

7 Remove the tacking from the corners of the blind, insert the lath and slipstitch the corners closed.

final touch

Add eyelets to the batten. Attach the blind, thread cord through the tape and eyelets, secure to an acorn, and trim the ends.

creating a *tile effect*

Large, flat surfaces are well suited to this technique. Use blue paint and the stencils will resemble the much-sought-after Delft tiles.

Create a tile effect with paint by using a special stencil. It is an unusual way to add colour and pattern to a surface. Apart from being attractive, it's also much easier to change the effect later – you simply paint over the stencilling to change both colour and pattern.

You need to work on a grid, and careful measuring and marking up are required to create the tile efffect. If working on a wall, use a plumb line and a spirit level to align the stencil tiles. An extra pair of hands is useful when using the plumb line to create the vertical lines – one person holds the plumb line in place while the other marks the surface.

GETTING STARTED

It is worth spending some time doing the measuring and marking as you can't change the grid once you've started stencilling the tiles. It is also worth doing a few stencils on a piece of scrap paper to check that you're not using too much paint, that the colour is suitable and that it creates the effect you want. You can do an accurate colour test by stencilling on scrap paper coloured or painted the same as that of the background you'll be working on.

USE THE TILE STENCIL • in kitchens and bathrooms • on roller blinds.

As the tile stencil probably won't fit the area to be stencilled exactly, decide where you want the complete tiles to fall and where you want to end with part of a tile. Stencil the whole tiles first and leave to dry. Then mask the stencil according to the gaps left and stencil these areas.

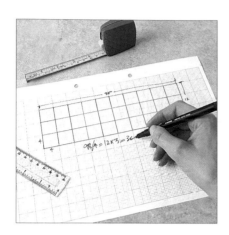

Crafty tip

Practise the stencilling on scrap paper before starting work on the real surface, so you can check how much paint to use and see how the design builds up into a tile effect.

1 Measure the surface to be stencilled. Working on graph paper, divide the surface area into a grid of squares that corresponds to the size of the stencil tiles you are using.

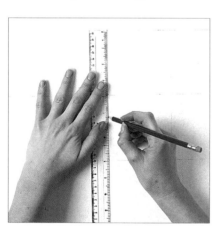

3 Complete the stencilling, and add authenticity to the design by drawing a grout line with a grey felt-tip pen (use a fabric pen if working on fabrics).

2 Transfer the plan to the actual surface with a pencil, using the plumb line for vertical lines and the spirit level for horizontal lines. Measure carefully so that all the squares are the same size. Do a test stencil and check for colour and the amount of paint. Start stencilling, doing alternate tiles, and leaving them to dry.

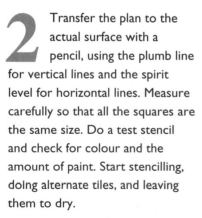

final touch

If you have used a felt-tip pen for the grouting and you intend varnishing the surface, spray it with aerosol fixative before you do so. This will prevent the felt-tip grouting effect from bleeding.

VARIATIONS

Use the tile outline to create the overall effect. The motif can be used on all the tiles or, as shown above, alternated to create a diagonal pattern.

Use the motif to create a border on the tile effect. This pattern is well suited to smaller areas.

On large areas, where the overall effect might be too much if all the tiles were stencilled, use the motif in groups to create a regular pattern.

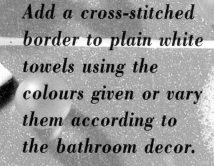

Add a cross-stitched border to plain white towels using the colours given or vary them according to the bathroom decor.

embroidered
TOWELS

You will need

WHITE GUEST TOWELS WITH A WOVEN BAND

TACKING THREAD IN A DARK COLOUR

WHITE 11 COUNT AIDA FABRIC

DMC STRANDED COTTON IN THE FOLLOWING COLOURS: BLUE 3807, LAVENDER 554, GREEN 3816

SIZE 24 TAPESTRY NEEDLE

SEWING NEEDLE

FUSIBLE BONDING WEB

Spend a little time sewing some embroidered borders on plain towels to liven up your bathroom. You can use toning or contrasting colours to tie in with the colour scheme. Although white towels were used here, you can use coloured ones instead. Match the embroidery thread to the decor or choose an assortment of toning colours for the cross-stitches.

The embroidery on the towels adds a special touch which will be appreciated by guests. They also make particularly attractive presents, to people who are setting up house or decorating a bathroom.

The borders are stitched on to specially woven fabric with obvious squares, designed for cross-stitch embroidery. The borders are backed with fusible bonding web to prevent fraying, then cut out leaving rows of a few squares on either side. The border is then bonded to the towel with a steam iron.

adding borders to towels

Embroidered borders add colour and pattern. To make the most economical use of the fabric, the embroidery isn't worked in a hoop.

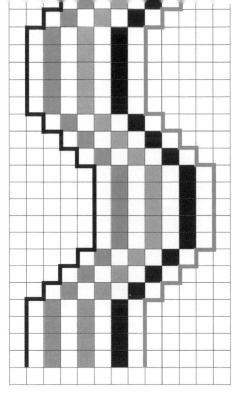

1 Measure the woven strip across the towels and add 1.2cm / ½in to the top and bottom. Mark two bands this size on the aida fabric with rows of tacking, positioning the bands side by side with at least 10 blocks in between. Find the centre of each band and mark with a few stitches.

2 Work the two geometric designs in cross-stitch from the chart using three strands of thread in the tapestry needle throughout. Work outwards from the centre, remembering that each coloured square on the chart represents one cross-stitch worked over one woven block of fabric.

3 At each end of the border, finish the stitching two or three blocks inside the tacked lines. Finish the borders by adding the linear details in backstitch, again using three strands of thread.

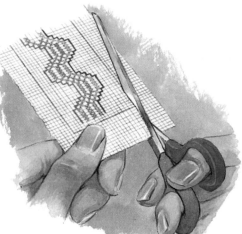

A. Cut out the border leaving a clear margin all round.

4 Press the embroidery lightly with a warm iron on the wrong side over a well-padded surface, taking care not to crush and flatten the stitches.

5 Following the manufacturer's instructions, iron a piece of fusible bonding web on to the back of the embroidery. When cool, cut out the bands allowing a margin of four unworked fabric blocks at the top and bottom of the band and two blocks at each end (A). For towels with very deep woven bands, allow extra fabric at the top and bottom, if necessary.

6 Peel away the backing paper of the fusible bonding web from the bands and position each one over the woven strip on the towels. Press the bands with a steam iron, or an ordinary iron and a damp cloth, to attach them.

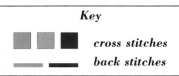

Key			
▨ ▨ ▨			*cross stitches*
▬ ▬ ▬			*back stitches*

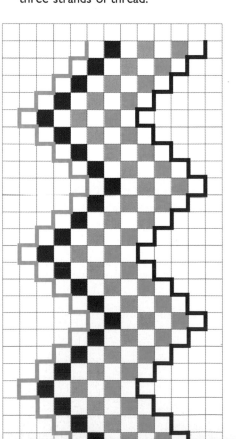

Crafty tip

For towels that are regularly machine washed, you can secure the embroidered strips with blanket stitch around the edge of the fabric with three strands of white thread.

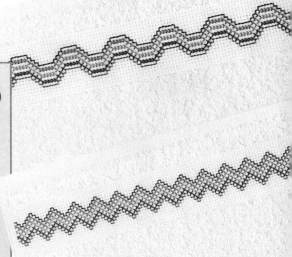

a drawstring
LINEN BAG

Fully reversible, this laundry basket liner is made using two different fabrics and can be used both ways. For convenience, the top is gathered with a drawstring.

This reversible laundry bag with its drawstring top is as useful as it is attractive. It will stop fragile items snagging on the sides of your basket and the drawstring top makes it easy to lift the bag from its container and simply carry it to the washing machine or laundromat. The sewing involved is straightforward once you have worked out a cutting plan. If your linen basket is not the same size as the one used here, follow the instructions but adapt the pattern to the size you require. Choose the fabric colours and pattern to complement your bathroom or bedroom, depending on where you keep your laundry basket.

OTHER SIZES

Although this bag is made specifically for a laundry basket, you can scale the pattern up or down to make any other drawstring bag. Adapt it into a small bag and you can use it for your make-up or toiletries, or into a larger version to use as a generous beach bag.

For the laundry or beach bag, use washable, shrink-resistant fabrics such as colour-fast cottons and towelling. If you adapt the pattern for a make-up bag, pick an elegant silk or satin.

179

making the linen bag

1 Measure your basket and draw a cutting plan on dressmakers' pattern paper to work out the lengths of fabric needed (A).

2 Iron the two lengths of fabric and place them right sides facing so that the selvedges match. Cut out the paper pattern pieces and pin them to the fabrics so that they lie parallel to the selvedges. Cut out the pieces through both thicknesses.

3 Put the two short sides of one rectangle together, right sides facing. Measure 10.5cm / 4¼in from the top edge. Mark this with a pin. Pin and stitch from the pin, leaving a seam allowance of 1.5cm / ½in. Iron the seam open and zigzag raw edges to the top. Fold back the unstitched tops to form a 1.5cm / ½in hem. Iron flat and top stitch (B).

4 Right sides facing, pin the bottom edge to the matching circle of fabric (C). Stitch, then iron seams open. Zigzag any raw edges. Repeat steps 3-4 with second fabric.

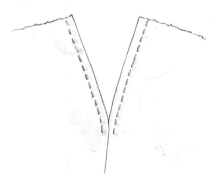

B. Top stitch the opening at the top of the side seam.

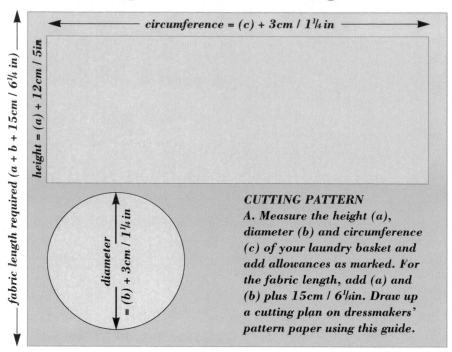

circumference = (c) + 3cm / 1¼in

height = (a) + 12cm / 5in

fabric length required (a + b + 15cm / 6¼ in)

diameter = (b) + 3cm / 1¼in

CUTTING PATTERN
A. Measure the height (a), diameter (b) and circumference (c) of your laundry basket and add allowances as marked. For the fabric length, add (a) and (b) plus 15cm / 6¼in. Draw up a cutting plan on dressmakers' pattern paper using this guide.

5 Put one bag into the other, right sides facing. Pin and sew the top edges together. Iron the seams open. Zigzag raw edges. Turn the bag the right way round, through the opening in the top. Iron the top edge.

6 Stitch through both thicknesses 9cm / 3½in down from the top edge to make a channel for the cord. As a guide, draw a line on a piece of masking tape stuck to the machine so that the line lies parallel to the foot, 9cm / 3½in from the needle (D). Sew each cord-end to stop fraying. Thread the cord through using a safety pin. Knot the ends together.

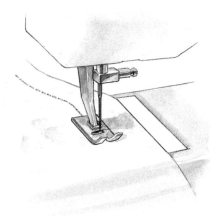

D. Stick masking tape on to the sewing machine surface to act as a guide when sewing the final seam.

Craftytip

If you need different-coloured threads for the top of the bag, use one shade for the shuttle and the other for the top spool.

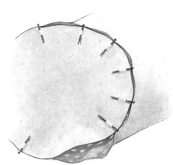

C. Divide the circle into sections and pin right sides facing.

crackle-glazed CABINET

Brighten up your bathroom – or any room you like – with this deceptively simple paint and varnish finish.

Crackle glaze can transform rather dull, everyday objects into eye-catching, stylish pieces that will enhance a room. The aged, cracked finish, caused by the action of varnish on paint, is particularly well suited to smallish wooden items. Use a piece of board or wood to experiment with different colour combinations and degrees of crackling (the thinner the layer of glaze, the more subtle the crackling will be). Make sure that the object you are working on is well sanded and thoroughly primed before applying any paint or crackle glaze.

decorating the cabinet

The green-cream effect works well in many bathroom settings, but you can of course choose any colours that complement or contrast with your bathroom decor. Try blue and white, or yellow for a touch of the seaside.

Craftytip

When applying the top coat over the crackle glaze, the brush must merely glide over the surface. A speedy, light touch will give a better finish.

1 Check the cabinet for any loose hinges or screws and replace them if necessary. Smooth the entire cabinet down with sandpaper. If the original paintwork on the cabinet is badly cracked or damaged, strip it down completely with liquid paintstripper, then sand down when dry.

2 Mask off the edges of the mirror (A), and apply a coat of primer or undercoat. Leave to dry. Sand the cabinet and apply a second coat of primer.

3 Apply your chosen base colour and leave to dry. This colour will show through as the colour of the crackles.

4 Apply the crackle glaze. The thickness of the glaze will determine the final look and texture of the crackle effect. Leave to dry. Apply the top coat of paint, in this case cream (B).

5 When dry, apply three coats of clear varnish to the cabinet, allowing it to dry between coats.

B. Apply a top coat of cream, using rapid, light strokes.

A. Attach the masking tape to the mirror to shield it from the paint.

welted CUSHION

Adding a gusset to a cushion cover allows you to fit it exactly and gives a neat tailored look to a seat.

You will need

PAPER AND PENCIL FOR TEMPLATE

TAPE MEASURE

SCISSORS

CUSHION FABRIC

FOAM CUSHION PAD

LINING FABRIC

40CM / 15¾IN ZIP

SEWING THREAD, NEEDLE AND PINS

IRON

SEWING MACHINE

PIPING CORD

CONTRAST BIAS BINDING

Cushions for window seats or wicker chairs usually have a tailored appearance with piped edges. Use piping cord and bias binding for this. You can make your own bias binding by cutting strips of fabric on the bias.

Foam in block form, which can be cut to shape, is used for the cushion. It has a depth of 5-10cm / 2-4in, so to make a tailored cover you need to make a welt or gusset running around the edge. You will also need a zip in the seam to remove the cover for washing.

If the cushion has a curved back and flat front, as here, include the zip in the back. Avoid making joins in the front of the welt, apart from at the corners. It is also best to cover the foam with a lining fabric – this helps the cover to lie smoothly and also protects the foam.

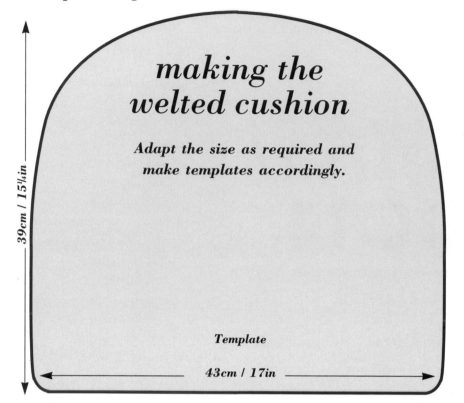

making the welted cushion

**Adapt the size as required and
make templates accordingly.**

Template

39cm / 15¼in

43cm / 17in

**B. Pin and tack the piping
covered with bias binding in place.**

1 Draw a template for the foam and fabric by placing a piece of paper on the seat of the chair and drawing round it. Cut out the template and check the fit – it shouldn't be too snug a fit. Use the template to cut two pieces of fabric, adding on 12mm / ½in for seam allowances. Cut the foam to size or ask the shop to do it for you. Check the depth – the foam used here is 7cm / 2¾in thick.

2 Cut the first strip of fabric for the welt to the same length as the zip – 40cm / 15¾in in this case – plus two times 12mm / ½in seam allowances, plus 2.5cm / 1in to allow for the zip insertion. Cut this strip in half lengthways. This is the width of the foam, plus four seam allowances (top, bottom, and either side of the zip).

3 Tack the corresponding long edges of the strip, right sides together taking a 12mm / ½in seam. Press open and insert the zip centrally, pinning, tacking and machine stitching it in place (A).

4 Cut a strip of fabric to the circumference of the cushion, less the length of the strip already cut, plus 12mm / ½in seam allowances at each end, and to the depth of the foam plus two times 12mm / ½in seam allowances.

5 Cut a length of piping to the circumference of the cushion, cover with bias binding and pin and tack around the seam line of the top of the cushion section, on the right side with raw edges together (B). Machine stitch in place using a zipper foot. Repeat the piping over the cushion section.

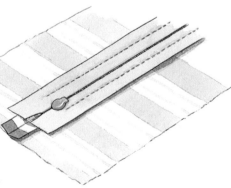

**A. Pin and tack the zip centrally
before machine stitching it in place.**

6 Join the welt sections, right sides together, tack and check they fit the foam snugly. Machine stitch and press the seams open.

7 With right sides together, pin, tack and machine the welt to the top cushion section, stitching close to the piping. Clip into the corners at the front.

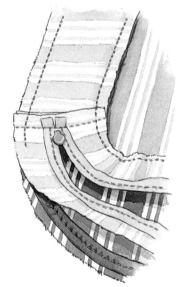

**C. Join the lower cushion section
to the welt, right sides together.**

8 Open the zip and attach the lower cushion section to the welt, right sides together (C). Machine stitch, clip the corners and turn through the zip. Make up the lining cover as for the top cover, but without the piping and the zip. Insert the foam and slipstitch the gap closed. Insert into the cushion cover and close the zip.

a seashell FRAME

Turn those sun-bleached shells you collected on holiday into a delightful frame – a year-round reminder of golden sands by the sea.

You will need

KITCHEN PAPER

TRAYS OR BAKING SHEETS
TO SORT SHELLS

A COLLECTION OF SHELLS

NEWSPAPER

FLAT WOODEN FRAME

2 TUBES OF ALL-PURPOSE
GEL GLUE

The lovely shells you couldn't resist picking up on the beach last year deserve better than being left and forgotten at the back of a cupboard. Why not put them to good use by making a pretty frame for a mirror or a photograph?

Shells come in all sorts of shapes and sizes, and colours vary from bone white to soft pinks and various shades of brown. Sort them according to their colour, shape and size, then work out a design. Aim for a simple, regular effect and do not use too many colours together.

CREATING THE DESIGN

Outline the frame on a piece of paper and use this as a template on which to arrange your shells. Regularity is the key. For a pleasantly graded result, use larger shells to cover the frame so that they form a scalloped effect along the outer edge. Place smaller ones neatly in a line along the inside edge to form a border.

Be sure your shells are clean. To get rid of any smell, soak them in a weak bleach solution, rinse and leave to dry.

You can fit a mirror in this shell frame and hang it in your bathroom or place it on your dressing table. Or you can use the frame to display your holiday photographs.

shell frame

Before you start, paint the frame white. Leave to dry. Paint the inside edge black. When dry, rub some gold finger paint over the black.

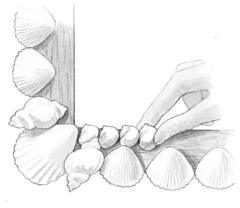

1 Put a sheet of kitchen paper on each tray and sort the shells according to size, shape and colour. Discard broken shells. Cut out a paper template of the frame and work out your design.

2 Protect your work surface with several layers of newspaper and place the frame in the centre.

3 Place a large shell in each corner and glue in position. Apply glue to the shell where it makes contact with the frame (A). Leave to dry.

4 Lay out some large shells along the outside edge of the frame so that they lie evenly and conceal the edge (B). When you are happy with the arrangement, glue them in position and leave to dry.

B. Arrange the larger shells so that they overlap and conceal the outside edge of the frame.

5 Using small shells, make a neat border along the inside edge of the frame (C). Arrange the shells in place before gluing them in position. Leave to dry.

6 Fill in the spaces in between, selecting shells according to their size and colour, and placing them so that they face in the same direction. Glue them in position. Fill in any remaining gaps with small shells and leave to dry.

C. Arrange the small shells so that they face in the same direction along the inside border.

Craftytip

If your frame is already fitted with a mirror, cover the mirror with kitchen paper to protect it from glue drips and to cushion the fall of any shells dropped on it.

With its subtle colouring and nautical theme, this frame is a perfect addition to the bathroom.

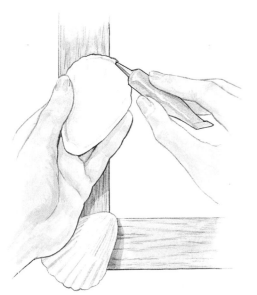

A. Apply the glue sparingly and only where the shell makes contact with the frame.

mutton cloth effects

*Use this soft knitted fabric to create
subtle paint effects in oil-based glazes
applied over a base coat of paint.*

Mutton cloth is also known as stockinette, and you can buy it from hardware shops and car accessory outlets. This inexpensive material is a loosely knitted fabric used for cleaning and polishing.

In this paint technique it is used to lift away glaze from an eggshell painted surface, leaving a faint impression of the weave of the cloth and a soft cloud-like appearance. You can carry on working the glaze to create an even softer appearance, but you will never achieve an even effect due to the fabric weave.

You will need to make up several pads of mutton cloth to work with – they become saturated with paint and you will find you are transferring paint to the surface rather than removing it. It is best to tear, rather than cut the mutton cloth, and to fold it so that all loose ends are tucked firmly into the centre, to avoid fluffs appearing on, and sticking to, the painted surface.

USE MUTTON CLOTH • to add a soft mottled finish to walls and ceilings • to decorate wooden furniture, such as chests of drawers.

Prepare the surface with a coat of eggshell paint, bearing in mind that the colour will show through the final glaze. Leave it to dry before applying the glaze.

1 Mix a glaze with oil-based paint (turquoise in this case), scumble glaze and a little white spirit, and paint the surface.

2 Make up a second glaze as above, using another colour (blue) and apply it over the first glaze immediately.

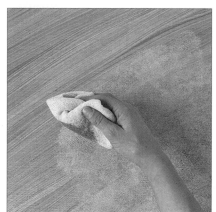

3 Tear a 30x50cm / 12x18in piece of mutton cloth by pulling a horizontal thread. Fold the edges to the centre, then the corners to hide all raw edges.

4 Work over the glazes with the mutton cloth pad using a dabbing action. The extent to which you blend the colours is entirely optional.

*Crafty*tip

Change the pad before it becomes saturated, bearing in mind the size of the pad will affect the final appearance – a large pad produces generous sweeps while a small pad gives a tighter finish.

VARIATIONS

Dark blue base coat with mid blue and turquoise glaze.

Pink base coat with a bright orange glaze.

Yellow base coat with orange glaze applied in patches.

Purple base coat with pink and mauve sweeps of glaze.

Green base coat with turquoise glaze applied in twists.

Pale pink base coat with dark pink glaze applied in sweeps.

painted cork printing

You can cut the end of a champagne or sparkling wine bottle cork to create a motif. Apply paint to the motif and use it to make repeat prints, randomly or in a regular pattern, on a surface.

Printing with corks allows you to produce small prints on a variety of surfaces. You must use champagne or sparkling wine corks as they are ejected, rather than pulled, from the bottle, and will therefore not be damaged by a corkscrew. The surface of the cork is sanded down, then the design is drawn on to the surface and it is cut out using a scalpel. Make vertical cuts, down into the cork, around the design first. Then cut in horizontally, from the sides, to remove the parts of the cork not needed for the design to create the raised image.

Apply paint to the cutout motif using a brush, then use the cork as a stamp to print the image. Renew the paint with each application to produce an even image.

USE CORK PRINTS • to decorate stationery and cards • to add colour and pattern to small areas.

If using more than one colour, do all the prints required in the one colour, clean the cork, and do the next one.

1 Sand the surface of the cork until it is flat, using medium-grade sandpaper.

2 Draw a design on the cork using a pencil, keeping the design as simple as possible.

3 Use a scalpel to cut down around the design for about 6mm / ¼in, keeping the cuts as straight as possible.

4 Cut in from the side to meet up with the vertical cuts and remove the pieces of cork not relevant to the design.

5 Use a small artist's paintbrush to apply emulsion paint on to the design, being careful not to add too much.

6 Apply the cork to the surface being decorated, adding more paint as you go.

Index